# The Wise Legacy

# By Daniel J. Siegel

*Cover Design by Bradley E. Siegel*

ISBN-13: 978-1507625590

ISBN-10: 1507625596

FIRST EDITION

# About the Author

Daniel J. Siegel graduated with honors in Government in 1981 from Franklin and Marshall College in Lancaster, Pennsylvania, yet another product of the Sid Wise legacy. As a freshman in the fall of 1977, Dan knew that he loved to write, and had thought about going to law school, but like most freshmen, he really did not have a grasp on his future. What he did have was a schedule that included a lab science that was primarily for pre-medical school students. Dan knew that course wasn't for him, so he went to see his pre-assigned freshman advisor, Sidney Wise. Dan explained that he needed to get out of the science course, and eventually Professor Wise agreed. More significantly, before Dan left Professor Wise's office, he had become a member of the staff of *The College Reporter*, F&M's weekly student-run newspaper. And Dan's life was about to change even more.

From that day on, in retrospect, it became clear that Professor Wise had a plan for Dan, not necessarily to set him on a career, but to allow him to develop his writing skills, skills that would eventually be the key to his success as a lawyer. By the time Dan had graduated from F&M, he was a "stringer," *i.e.,* a part-time writer for Lancaster's morning newspaper, *The Intelligencer Journal,* and had honed his writing skills even more. Dan then enrolled and graduated from Temple University School of Law in 1984 and set out on a career as a lawyer. Dan became known for his writing skills, and was fortunate to serve as counsel on many successful appeals, primarily in the areas of personal injury and workers' compensation litigation. Dan also learned that he loved technology, which he discovered when he authored his Honors thesis at F&M in 1981. Dan took that interest and became known to many as the "Geek Lawyer" (if you search that term in Google Images, Dan's is one of the first pictures you will see). In 2005, Dan opened his own law firm and a technology consulting firm for lawyers, both in Havertown (Delaware County, Pennsylvania), where he has served since 2008 as a Haverford Township Commissioner. In that position, Dan has developed a reputation as a bipartisan official who works well with his colleagues, regardless of party affiliation; in other words, Dan aspires to be the type of elected official who tries to do what is right, not what is politically expedient. He has been credited with bringing the Township technologically into the 21st Century and with creating a remarkable level of transparency in local government.

Dan continues to practice law, play with technology, and serve as a Haverford Township Commissioner. He also has written numerous books, including *How to Do More in Less Time: The Complete Guide to Increasing Your Productivity and Improving Your Bottom Line; Checklists for Lawyers; Pennsylvania Workers' Compensation Law: The Basics – A Primer for New Lawyers, General Practitioners & Others* (now in its second edition); *Android Apps in One Hour for Lawyers*; and, *Changing Law Firms: Ethical Guidance for Pennsylvania Law Firms and Attorneys* (now in its second edition). Dan is also a frequent writer and lecturer on a wide range of topics, but he is of course most passionate about *The Wise Legacy*.

Dan is married to Eileen Watts Siegel, who is Chair of the English Department at Kohelet Yeshiva High School in Merion, Pennsylvania. He has two sons, Bradley, a woodworker and product designer, and

Douglas, who is currently a student at Franklin and Marshall College. Douglas' middle name, Steven, was chosen in memory of Sid Wise.

The search for more of Sid Wise's legacies continues. If you have any comments about the book, are or know a Sid Wise legacy, please feel free to contact Dan Siegel. You can reach him at dan@sidwisebook.com or phone (610-446-7614) or mail (1705 Marilyn Drive, Havertown, PA 19083).

# Dedication

So many people can credibly say that they are who they are because of Sid Wise. I am but one of many of his legacies, and certainly not the most prominent or most accomplished. What I am is a better person, a better father, a better commissioner, and a better lawyer, all because Sid touched my life. In fact, this book demonstrates how Sid not only touched my life, but how he continues to influence it. So while the subject of this book is Sid Wise, so is the person who inspired not only this book, but also so much of my life.

Sid, thank you for taking an interest in a poor freshman who knew he didn't belong in a science course for pre-meds, and thank you for making me realize that, while politics is the art of the possible, so is life itself. Thank you Sid for everything.

# Contents

3

# Introduction

Writing a book about former Franklin and Marshall College Government Professor Sidney Wise is a labor of love that became a passion. For nearly five years, I traversed the country meeting with Sid's students, colleagues and friends. Notice that I did not use the word "former" to describe these people. The reason is simple and astounding – when you mention the name Sid Wise, doors open, emotions spill out and people begin discussing their relationship with this very special man as though the events happened yesterday. But they did not. Instead, Sid's impact on people was so strong and so indelible that their past remains the present.

Who are these people? They are political leaders, they are judges, they are people at the forefront of whatever career they have chosen. And for each, the choice was facilitated by one man, Sid Wise, their college Government professor. Wise had the uncanny ability to see in his students what many of them did not see in themselves. And his students trusted him, and accept his suggestions. The results are clear – his legacies have changed the country and continue to do so, roughly two decades after Sid's death. That is the "Wise legacy."

So what is this book, and why did I write it?

When I graduated from Franklin and Marshall College in Lancaster, Pennsylvania in 1981, I knew that Sid was special and that he had a tremendous impact on my life. But as I grew older, I came to realize and appreciate his impact not only on me, but also on the country he loved, and on all of the students who were his second family.

Then I attended an F&M alumni event, a forum that was held in Philadelphia to discuss the 2008 Presidential election. Moderated by pollster G. Terry Madonna, the event featured F&M alumni Ken Duberstein, Bill Gray, Stanley Brand, and Ken Mehlman. The event was designed to be an analysis of the upcoming election, but it turned into a moving tribute by each panelist to the spirit and inspiration of Sid Wise.

For many years, I had been saying that someone needed to write the biography of this man who touched so many. However, it became clear that evening that if I did not write the book, no one would. As soon as this thought struck me, I turned to Catherine Jasons, another F&M alum whom I met through Sid's network, and said that I was going to write this book. I, of course, had no idea of the magnitude of the project, but I was determined to complete it.

I quickly learned that some of Sid's colleagues and students had passed away, and that others were in poor health. I endeavored to meet as many of these people as possible so that I could tell the world about this man, not through my eyes, but through the words of some of the many people he touched. It took many years to meet with all of the people who bring these pages to life. And there are others I was not able to meet with, yet still hope to do so.

What amazed me was one simple fact: No matter whom I contacted, and despite the fact that virtually none of the people in this book knew me, every one of them opened their doors – and their hearts – to me, willingly and without hesitation. The result is the stories that follow.

What I have done is to allow the interviewees' stories to speak for themselves. Other than some minor editing for clarity and readability, what you have here is a verbatim compilation of the love and reverence that so many people have for one man. What you also have is a tribute to the power of a teacher.

Christa McAuliffe said that "I touch the future. I teach." This book is about a teacher who not only touched the future, he changed it. Sid always knew which buttons to push, and how to inspire students and colleagues to reach levels they never realized they could attain. He not only instilled confidence in his students, he helped them discover their inner strengths and allowed them to foster their leadership skills. That is truly the "Wise Legacy," inspiring others to reach inside themselves, to discover their most important skills, to become leaders, and to use those skills to help others, always in a civil and caring manner.

But first an overview.

# Tribute To Dr. Sidney Wise, Charles A. Dana Professor Of Government, Franklin And Marshall College – Hon. William H. Gray III (Extension of Remarks – May 04, 1989)

[Page: E1531]

## HON. WILLIAM H. GRAY III
## in the House of Representatives

*THURSDAY, MAY 4, 1989*

Mr. GRAY. Mr. Speaker, I rise today to share with the Members of this House the outstanding accomplishments of Dr. Sidney Wise, Charles A. Dana Professor of Government at Franklin and Marshall College. As he retires from 37 years of teaching and researching about the Congress, the legislative process, and the American political system, it is fitting that we pay tribute to him.

Dr. Wise's interest in politics was whetted in his undergraduate years at Harvard College where he graduated cum laude in 1948. Upon the completion of a Ph.D. in public law in 1952, Professor Wise joined the faculty of Franklin and Marshall College and went on to build one of the most distinguished faculty records in the history of that 200-year-old college.

From the beginning of his career, Dr. Wise devoted himself to teaching an appreciation of the role of the politician in our society. And his purpose? To make students realize the nobility of public service and the vital role that political action plays in our democracy. Given this philosophy, Professor Wise's students quickly find themselves immersed in the transcripts of hearings, in dialogs with politicians and other political actors, and in developing a capacity to read commentaries about politics with political sophistication.

This hands-on, observation-and-involvement approach has led hundreds of his students into the halls of government over the past 30 years. Professor Wise was in fact one of the founders in creating political internships which now place thousands of students throughout our local, State, and National Governments. In the early 1960's, Professor Wise worked with the Citizenship Clearing House Foundation in persuading frequently reluctant Pennsylvania Congressmen and Senators to take college students as summer interns. Today, there is probably no congressional office that is without an intern in any month of the year.

Throughout his career, Professor Wise has always informed his teaching with both scholarly and political activity. Always believing that the theory in scholarly journals should be informed by practice, Professor Wise quickly immersed himself in Democratic politics in Lancaster, PA, the home of Franklin and Marshall College. One of his early successes was the election of the first Democratic mayor of the city of Lancaster since the Great Depression. Several years later, he was successful in getting the first Democratic legislator elected by a hairline majority in that traditionally Republican city. And through this activity in politics at the local and State level, Dr. Wise made contacts in both parties which provided speakers and sources of internships for his students.

Professor Wise's scholarly activity has blended academic theory with the practical problems facing politicians. In 1964, Dr. Wise spent a sabbatical year working as a legislative assistant for Senator Joseph Clark of Pennsylvania. During that year and subsequently, he collaborated in researching and writing `Congress: The Sapless Branch,' which presented Senator Clark's attack on what he saw as the lacidness of the Senate, and a later work, `Congressional Reform: Problems and Prospects.' As a spinoff from his work with Senator Clark, Dr. Wise collaborated with a colleague, Dr. Richard Schier, in publishing two books that gathered together seminal articles on the Congress and the Presidency. Professor Wise's interest in using public policy questions to illustrate and illuminate the nature of politics led him to publish an annual series of issues which presented opposing points of view on current political issues. Since the seventies, Dr. Wise has broadened his research interests to include the Pennsylvania State Legislature. For that body, he developed a program of seminars for freshmen legislators and, in 1984 he published a definitive work entitled `The Legislative Process of Pennsylvania.'

But the greatest contributor of Professor Wise lies in the thousands of students he has touched through the decades and in the hundreds of students he has encouraged to enter the public service. At present, there are over 145 of Dr. Wise's students working in Washington. And according to a New York Times article, Professor Wise's network is perhaps one of the largest in the Nation's Capital.

Perhaps most notable among this net is former White House Chief of Staff, Kenneth Duberstein who said this of his former teacher:

He was a rare teacher who talked about the day-in, day-out process of governing, putting coalitions together, making government work. When I was in the White House, I would call him periodically when I needed advice from someone not inside the Beltway.

But, Mr. Speaker, I must face up to being part of the Wise network for I, myself, was an undergraduate at Franklin and Marshall College. Thus, I can personally testify that Sid Wise changed my life. He encouraged me to get in to public policy, and he was responsible for my first hands-on political experience. In fact, my interest in the vocation of politics stemmed from the summer when, at Professor Wise's urging, I took an internship in the office of my predecessor in the early 1960's.

Mr. Chairman, Dr. Sidney Wise represents the highest ideal of the small college teacher, the teacher committed to working closely and intimately, carefully and caringly, with young people seeking to understand and make sense out of the world around him. Thirty-seven years ago, Professor Wise went into college teaching because he believed that one could make a life in educating the young, making them deeper and more sophisticated thinkers and citizens. For Sidney Wise college teaching is a vocation and a calling.

In saluting him today, we pay tribute to all such men and women who chose teaching as a vocation. For it is they who mediate and direct the changes that education makes in our lives. We salute them all, for truly, they are the carriers of our civilization.

# About Sid Wise

"The greatest good you can do for another is not just share your riches, but reveal to them their own"

Benjamin Disraeli

We define most people based on when they were born, what their job was, and when they died. Sid Wise was born on July 13, 1924 in Massachusetts and died on February 15, 1994 in Florida. Dr. Wise received his bachelor's degree *cum laude* from Harvard College in 1948 and his doctor of philosophy degree from the University of California at Los Angeles in 1952. Attending college was not always in the cards, and also helps explain why Sid Wise cared so much about creating opportunities for others.

According to Sid's son David, "It was very touch-and-go whether Sid was even going to go to college. He graduated very high in his high school class, but it looked like he was going to have to go to work because his family was in pretty bad shape – it was just his mother and his sister. One of his guidance counselors in high school, in Lynn High School said, 'What are you doing next year, Sid,' and he goes, 'Well, I don't know, probably going to help my uncle out in a store, blah,

blah, blah, you know,' 'Are you out of your mind?' and he goes, 'You're going to college.'"

"That counselor was someone like my dad of that generation. He pushed him into going to Harvard, and he got on that streetcar every day and schlepped over from Lynn to Cambridge, one year before he went into the Army. So someone pushed him too. I wondered sometimes if that didn't have an impact on his thinking that here was someone who got me on the road."

Wise joined the faculty of Franklin and Marshall College in 1952 and retired in· 1989 as Charles A. Dana Professor of Government. After his retirement, he served as a volunteer fund-raiser for the college, working in the alumni programs and development office. He received the Lindback Foundation Teaching Award in 1965. Previously, he was a Ford Foundation Fellow and served in a Legislative Service Fellowship Program with the Commonwealth of Pennsylvania American Political Science Association from 1969 to 1971.

But this description does not capture Sid Wise at all. To the contrary, it is through the accomplishments of his colleagues and students that Sid Wise is best known. Wise's students, of course, have become known not only because of their positions but also because of the network of internships and other opportunities he fostered. According to longtime colleague, and "partner in crime" John Vanderzell, Wise's path to F&M was the result of networking by F&M Professor Glenn Schubert, who left the College and went to UCLA, where he met Sid Wise. According to Vanderzell, "the Dean here asked Schubert who he would recommend to take his, Schubert's, place, and he recommended Sidney highly.

So Sidney came on Schubert's recommendation, and they then needed another person. So Schubert called Syracuse and Syracuse said that I would be a good person to be with Sidney. So I got the appointment after Sidney did and we came in the same year, in 1952."

While he is unsure of how the internship idea got its start, Vanderzell believes "that maybe Sidney had that either in his genes or implanted at UCLA. [In addition, the] first full summer that Sidney was here, he somehow managed to become an assistant or an intern to Mayor Kendig Bare of Lancaster."

"Kendig Bare was a Republican mayor of Lancaster," says Vanderzell. "Bare may have been the only kind of liberal Republican that had ever seen the inside of a governmental institution in Lancaster County. Sidney, however he made that contact, apparently persuaded Bare that he, Sidney, would be of value to him over the summer as his kind of assistant, his Man Friday, whatever, so that Bare could, if he wanted to, go on vacation for a while. So one could say that Sidney was the first intern in the City."

Vanderzell also recalls that "Sidney developed a relationship with a person at Rutgers. Rutgers Public Affairs Program thought that it was churning out people who would become the career administrative people who would be second in command to political people, the Chiefs of Staff and that type of thing. Sidney sent some students to Rutgers for graduate work in that area." Thus, while Sidney was a Democrat, "What mattered to him was getting students placed where they would have a sense of what public and political life was all about."

No matter how they met, colleagues and students remember those moments. D. Grier Stephenson Jr., who succeeded Wise as the Charles A. Dana Professor of Government, recalls first meeting Wise in September 1969, when he "was in the Army and on the job market, at the American Political Science Association was meeting in New York. [At the time] Franklin and Marshall had advertised a vacancy to take the position that was vacated when John Vanderzell became Dean of the College. I applied for that position. Dick Schier, chair of the Department, had contacted me and we arranged to meet in New York at the APSA convention."

"I met Dick and Sidney for lunch. We sat down and Dick started asking me some questions relating to political science or something. Sidney injected and wanted to know which films I had seen and the rest of the conversation had to do with movies, had to do with film and we didn't talk much about the position at all. I thought later that since – I enjoy movies and film, but not like Sidney did – that I probably came very close to missing out on a good job because that's clearly what Sidney was interested in. You would have thought they were interviewing me for a position in film, not for a position in political science." That meeting highlighted Wise's love of both politics and cinema, two areas that dominated his life.

Of course, Professor Stephenson was hired and attributes his success and longevity as a professor to his colleague. "I find it difficult to understand how I could have lasted very long as a college teacher without Sidney. He was the sort of person who took a particular interest in people – he wanted to know what you were doing, but he was never pushy, but he wanted to make sure that you knew that he was there, that you could

15

talk to him and he liked for you to talk to him and bounce things off him. I just found him an amazing person in terms of insight, ideas, his knowledge, his judgment. I just found him magnetic."

Wise also helped his colleagues develop professionally. "He was just a remarkable person like that. On campus, he not only knew everybody but, of course, everybody knew who he was. People would seek him out for advice and they'd want to know what he thought. He wielded really a tremendous influence on campus because people respected his judgment."

"He would talk about politics," Stephenson recalls, but "he wouldn't talk about his politics, so that you really would have to talk a fair amount with Sidney before you necessarily knew how he felt about something. He frowned upon and made very, very clear to the junior members of the department that the classroom lectern was not a pulpit, that you weren't in there to win students over to your particular perspective. You were in there to win them over to the idea of studying government and politics, to excite them about that, not about being liberal, conservative, Democrat or Republican, because he was as open to students who were Republicans as he was to students who were Democrats, even though he was very much a Democrat himself."

Alan Glazer, the Henry P. and Mary B. Stager Professor of Business at F&M, and a 1969 graduate of the College, joined the F&M faculty in 1975 after receiving his Ph.D. from the University of Pennsylvania. Although he never took any courses with Professor Wise, he recalls that when he joined the faculty, "Sid and [other members of the faculty] did a lot of hands on mentoring. It was the kind of place where a lot of that was done in a small personal way with dinners at people's homes."

Glazer notes that Sid "produced folks who had often very successful careers above and beyond what might have been expected with a different kind of education." As a colleague, he notes that Sid's "heart was in the right place. This was a guy who would give you whatever time and energy you needed. What I do remember vividly is the way the faculty got its business done when I first joined. The faculty then was mostly men who moved to Lancaster generally right out of PhD programs with their spouses, who gave up their careers to come here and start a family, because that's what was expected when I came in the mid-70s."

"We met at the AAUP meeting on a regular basis. I think it was once a month, and Sid was always there. The younger faculty were always in attendance. Over beer, pretzels and chips, the work of the faculty got done. He exercised his political savvy in that kind of setting. It was a consensus building process, and the consensus building was done in a very informal friendly way and when the decisions needed to be made it was a very efficient process. I think Sid made it very easy to contribute and get stuff done."

Rose Musser, the long-time secretary of the Government Department, remembers Sid's focus on students. "He was just such a warm caring person. The biggest thing that I remember about him is how it was so important for him to follow through with the students after they left the college. He wanted everybody to have a job. They got calls from him all the time; he was the ultimate networker. He was on the phone all the time, trying to find internships, jobs. That's just what he did besides teaching."

"Any time there was a note about anybody in the newspaper," she recalls, "we'd always have to cut it out and put it in that student's file. As long as he was there, the files were complete, because he was very, very serious about that. He always followed through with those students. I mean you didn't just leave the college and you were gone. If you had any connection with him at all he followed your career."

Long-time colleague Robert Gray, The Honorable and Mrs. John C. Kunkel Professor of Government at F&M, has similar memories. "He was as warm to his colleagues as he was to everyone else. But there's never been anyone who focused as much attention on students while they were here and after they graduated as he did. He was just an extremely unique individual with the amount of time he had to, and was willing to devote to that."

In a February 23, 1987 article in the *New York Times*,[1] Martin Tolchin (who also founded *The Hill* and *Politico*), noted that Bill Gray was one of 145 former students who then worked for the Federal Government in Washington, noting that Wise "believes in the flesh-and-blood approach to government and politics and decries what he considers the current fashion in political science: a fascination with computers instead of people." His legacy lives through that flesh and blood.

---

[1] "Washington Talk: Professor Peoples the Bureaucracy," by Martin Tolchin, *The New York Times*, February 23, 1987.

# John H. Vanderzell – A Partner in Crime

Emeritus Professor of Government and former Dean of the College John Vanderzell was also known as one of the three "partners in crime" who, along with Sid Wise and Richard Schier ("the Big Three"), helped to foster the interconnections between Government students, alumni, government and business. Together, these three men guided countless students into their careers, always seeing and cultivating their students' potential.

Vanderzell joined the Government Department in the early 1950s, shortly after Wise joined the faculty. They decided to rename the department "Government," and began laying the foundation for one of the College's most enduring legacies. As noted in one article, "Although The Big Three, as they came to be known, were the only Government faculty throughout the next decade, their influence was felt across campus and beyond ... because they infused political science theory with real-world insights gained from their own involvement in local, state and federal government. Wise and Schier were both legislative assistants to U.S. Senator Joseph Clark. Vanderzell was active in both state and local government."

Vanderzell recalls Sid Wise as "a raconteur of enormous dimensions. He was just a grand person. To know Sidney was to love him." But while all of them "emphasized human relationships, they knew that political science would increasingly be driven by numbers. [As a result,] they instituted a required course in research methods and statistics."

Although Sid Wise "was appointed to the faculty first, I arrived on campus first. I came and I actually taught a summer session in '52. Sid didn't come on campus until the beginning of the fall semester in '52."

"Sidney was the second Jewish professor," Vanderzell recalls. "Jake Freedman was the first, except Sid wasn't observant. He was nonetheless a member of the clan. Jewish students flocked to Sidney like flies to honey. I think students would have flocked to Sidney whether he were Jewish or Gentile or Arabian. He was a father figure, I think, for a lot."

"During the season of our discontent, the late '60s, there was lots of dissent and a lot of students were having a lot of fun with that dissent. One of the really smart-alecky dissenters was a Jewish student. Sidney called him into the office and told him that if he didn't change his ways, he was going to call his mother. And that fixed it."

Vanderzell acknowledges that there are many "Sid Wise stories." Perhaps one of the *best* is the story of Sidney and Eleanor Roosevelt. Shortly after they joined the faculty, "Eleanor Roosevelt was coming to Lancaster at the invitation, I think, of the local Chamber of Commerce, but not a college organization. Eleanor was scheduled to have dinner at the Hamilton Club either before or after the presentation that she was to make. Sidney, and I'm not sure who else, intercepted Eleanor Roosevelt in Coatesville. Sidney wanted to advise Eleanor that the club admitted neither Jews nor blacks, and maybe Eleanor wouldn't want to patronize the Hamilton Club for that reason. And sure enough, Eleanor didn't."

**Sid Wise and Eleanor Roosevelt**

But it remains Wise's ability to spot students with potential that was his greatest legacy, "to the Sidney genius," as he puts it. The other aspect of the "Sidney genius" was the effort to make the Government Department a major department at the College, especially for non-science students. "Before the government department, [and] allow me to use the expression that characterized us, before the Big Three, the History Department was the big department in the social sciences. Frankly, it wasn't very good. We determined that we would be as good as we possibly could be. That meant our hires would be very, very good. We worked on our connections with graduate schools and professional schools, and we thought that the standards that we set would be recognized. Whether that would happen, of course we didn't know, but gradually, and then not so gradually, it just caught on."

"Then we became the pre-law department and that was very attractive. Frankly, I think the department did hire really exciting people, beginning with Stan Michalak, Grier Stephenson and Joe Karlesky. I just think that's what happened."

Wise also acquired significant power within the College. Vanderzell also recalls that Sidney was elected President of the College Chapter of the American Association of University Professors three consecutive times. He used that position to be "kitchen cabinetesque in most regimes, probably especially beginning with Frederick de Wolfe Bowman, the first College President who expressly identified the goal of making F&M a national institution rather than merely a regional institution."

When recalling his colleague, Vanderzell notes that "he was a guy to whom people were attracted like bees to honey – for all the right reasons. There was no expectation of special favors. But there was an expectation of due regard. I think that to know Sidney was to love him."

# David Wise – A Legacy of Service

Sid Wise's son, David, has a unique perspective on his father's life and influence. The younger Wise's career as a public servant also demonstrates the extent of that influence. As a Director of the U.S. Government's General Accountability Office's Physical Infrastructure team, Wise oversees a variety of federal agencies and other entities to help Congress to ensure the continued efficiency, safety, and security of the nation's transportation systems, telecommunications networks, oil and gas pipelines, and federal facilities. In other words, Wise is responsible for helping to assure that the federal government provides the services it is supposed to and utilizes its facilities as efficiently as possible to save taxpayer dollars.

"I've always been in public service," Wise notes. He first worked for the GAO in the early 1980s, spent a few years in Washington, and four years in the GAO office in Hawaii. He returned to Washington and moved to the Inspector General's office in the Department of State, which is that agency's version of the GAO, and rose through the ranks. Needing a change of pace, Wise joined the Foreign Service and moved to Vietnam, serving as a political officer at the embassy. He next moved to Laos, where he ran the U.S. counter-reconnaissance program. Before returning to the U.S., Wise agreed to work in a provincial reconstruction team in Afghanistan, and spent a year in Helmand Province with an Army Reconstruction and Civil Affairs Team as its political advisor, traveling with the team on missions, performing "governance" activities, and working with the local population. After returning to the U.S., Wise entered the GAO's executive training program, and now serves as a Director of the Physical Infrastructure Team.

Wise's youth was not typical. He recalls having political meetings at home. "Democratic politics, there would be various strategy meetings, that kind of stuff. They occurred on a semi-regular basis when there was an election coming, or there was some kind of event going on. To have all these meetings in your house [left a strong impression]. [In addition], Dad was kind of active in civil rights stuff in the early days, so there was some activity with that. I remember James Farmer coming, and that was a pretty big deal. I think he came to do something at F&M, and he stopped at our house and spent a couple of hours talking over local issues." Farmer was a civil rights activist who was one of the organizers of the Freedom Riders, who rode interstate buses in the South to test conditions after the Supreme Court ruled that racial segregation in public transportation was illegal because it violated the Interstate Commerce Act.

"It was hard not to be influenced by those things when you see, as a kid, someone like James Farmer in your living room talking about civil rights issues. This was before the Civil Rights Bill was passed. Also, there was always a constant stream of books, magazines, newspapers, and Dick Schier is over there on Sunday afternoon and they're reading *The New York Times* to each other – it's hard not to be impacted by that," Wise recalled.

"But Lancaster was," he notes, "a very segregated place at one time. You know, no blacks were allowed, for example, at a couple of public swimming pools. I don't know if it was explicitly written in the laws, but it was sort of an informal enforcement. The Maple Grove, which doesn't exist anymore, was always known as a place where blacks were not welcome. Then Dad was involved. I can remember also a few labor issues, there were some kind of strikes somewhere, and we were going into the store, and he said, 'No, we're not crossing that picket line.' He felt very strongly about those kinds of issues, because he had grown up in a working class environment."

In addition, Wise recalled his father's desire to help students. "I think his view was basically that the primary purpose for kids coming to college was to have an education, and that some things served as needless distractions. But if he saw that a kid, no matter who he was, was interested and was engaged, he would go the full nine yards for him. When we used to go to a lot of away football games, he'd always have a couple of kids in the car. He'd invite somebody to come along. If he believed that one of the kids that he taught was fairly promising, he engaged them, asking what are you going to be doing, what are you thinking about – I think they felt it was a great honor to be cooped up in the car and at a football game for a couple of hours, but every time we went on the road, there'd be one or two students with us."

According to the younger Wise, the most lingering aspect of his father's influence was his ability to connect people. "His style of networking was remarkable, and he never failed to find a connection; then the whole thing would just keep growing and growing and growing.

Of course, the younger Wise recalls the "Eleanor Roosevelt story." "Eleanor Roosevelt was coming to

Lancaster," he remembers. "She was to speak at the Hamilton Club downtown. At that time, the Hamilton Club had no Jewish or African-American members, and its membership was strictly the old line Lancaster business aristocracy kind. When Sid heard that she was coming, he got on the phone and called somebody who was apparently helping to arrange this or knew her, and explained the story, and she immediately dropped the plan to speak. She did come to Lancaster, but she spoke somewhere else."

# Joel Ervin – "He Saved My Life"

Society often stereotypes people based on circumstances, rather than their abilities and qualifications. For Joel Ervin, a divorced mother in the 1950s, her life came to be defined by her marital status, making it difficult for her to find a job. That is, until she met Sid Wise, who "saved her life." "He was such a nice man, such a decent human being," she explained. "There was a charisma, and how do you explain that? You just don't. Just some people have it, some people don't."

"I believe it was in 1957 or the spring of '58. I was a part-time secretary for four different departments," says Ervin. "Then I got a call from Eileen Wise to ask me if I was looking for work, and I was. I was young, I was the mother of two children and divorced. I had a college degree but I could not get a job anywhere doing anything. In those days, if you were young and had two children, you were considered unreliable, irresponsible, instead of thinking, *'Well, of course, she's responsible, she's taking care of two children and trying find a job.'* At any rate, that's the way it was, and Sid knew me because I had been up at Eileen's helping her work on some Democratic material, stuffing envelopes and things like that.

"So, I went up [to F&M] and he and I shared an office on the first floor of Old Main. That was my first job with him, and I was so impressed because he was kind to me and gave me a job. My confidence was not very high because I was going through a divorce that hadn't been finalized yet, but he changed my life because he gave me the job. As far as I'm concerned, he saved my life. I didn't know what I was going to do and

27

maybe that sounds dramatic, but that's the way it was. I had no sisters, no brothers, and no cousins. I had my mother and father in Harrisburg. No money or anything. I had nobody down here, so he saved my life."

"I was part-time and at the end of the spring semester. I remember saying, 'Well Sid, this is my last day here, I'm going to be leaving now, my last day is supposed to be the 31st.' 'What? You're leaving?' I said, 'Yes, that's as long as I'm supposed to work.' He went back and he got Dick Schier and John Vanderzell. He said, 'Wait here a minute, wait here, just don't go yet.' They went down to Old Main and talked to who was in charge of hiring and firing, the personnel director. Probably fifteen or twenty minutes later, I looked out the back window and there were the three of them coming up toward my office. I saw them in the window of Sid's office and my office. They came up into my office and said, 'Well, we got you a job. Yes, you're going to start full-time and your salary is $3,000 a year.' I was thrilled to death. So that's how I became their full-time secretary, and it just kept getting better and better and better."

"I was terribly in awe of all three of them. Sid was kind, Dick Schier was funny, John Vanderzell was very, very nice and helpful. I stayed there for 12 years. When I went there at the beginning [it was] the three of them, and I believe there were 12 government majors."

"I had a safe haven up in the Government Department and I got anything I wanted up there. Before you knew it, I had a red Selectric typewriter, which I didn't want, but which they wanted me to have, so they let me pick a color. I can't tell you what a wonderful sense of satisfaction and trust. I stayed with the Government Department, and Sid made sure that I got a decent raise. It's not that I asked for it, it just seems like anything I wanted I could get. Colored paper, a new mimeograph machine, a new typewriter, filing cabinets. It really did seem like he was so respected on that campus, and he had a way to get just about anything."

Of course, Ms. Ervin noted Sid Wise's ever-growing influence. "He was very, very much respected, and fun to be around. He could go down and just talk to anybody. He was able to communicate with politically affiliated alumni by the sheer power of his personality and what he had to offer, that 'if you can take an intern in your office, that would be good for your constituents back home, and be good for you because you might get an invitation from Franklin and Marshall.' That kind of conversation is so typical of him."

"Sid changed my life, my children's life," she summarized. "I had never been an intolerant person, but I was raised in an intolerant family and when the Civil Rights movement started, with the Vietnam War going on, the stuff with Nixon, those men, especially Sid, were all involved in that. So, consequently, I became more involved – it was such a radical change in my life because of him. It's astounding, even to this day, I just can't imagine what my life would have been like if I hadn't met him. I mean that from the bottom of my heart."

# Judge Ronald Buckwalter – "He Made Me Think Government Was Worthwhile"

Federal judges rule on a wide range of cases from criminal matters to Constitutional challenges, and a whole host of other disputes. Regardless of the type, Federal court cases can have great public importance and garner significant media attention, so judges must be willing to rule without concern for public opinion or media fallout. After a quarter century on the bench, Ronald Buckwalter, a Senior Judge in the Eastern District of Pennsylvania, is no stranger to such cases. For example, Judge Buckwalter has presided over lawsuits involving the eviction of Boy Scouts troops because of their refusal to allow gays to join, challenges to the constitutionality of NCAA rules, and the corruption trial of Pennsylvania State Senator Vincent Fumo, which is perhaps the most publicized case of the jurist's career, in which his sentence was subject to praise and highly vitriolic criticism.

Judge Buckwalter has never shied away from making tough, and sometimes extremely unpopular, rulings. For example, in the Fumo case, the Judge's sentence was called a "travesty" by prosecutors, and some members of the press and the public. Others applauded the judge for refusing to bow to media pressure and for sentencing the convicted official based upon what the judge believed was the right decision rather than what the media and others thought was appropriate.

But being the center of controversy, and ruling upon matters of public import, was far from Judge

Buckwalter's mind when the Lancaster native enrolled at F&M in 1954. Then he met Professor Wise. "One thing about Sid was – he just opened a door to the real world. You have to understand the background. Most of us were from Lancaster at that time or from surrounding counties. We were small town people, small county people. This guy was out of our league totally. I knew that at the time, and probably didn't realize until later how much out of our league Sid was at that time. But to his credit, he was able to teach us," Buckwalter recalled.

Buckwalter "had him for government. At that time we had Saturday morning classes. He was probably the only professor that could keep you awake during the Saturday morning class. His approach to things made me think that government was a worthwhile venture, no question about it, because he had that genuine excitement and interest in it. Not many professors can convey that," said Buckwalter.

Professor Wise had a direct impact on the young student. "It's hard to say that he inspired me, but he made me really like government and think it was worthwhile." Judge Buckwalter's relationship with Professor Wise expanded after he graduated. He recalls, for example, that in 1969, he was City Chairman for the campaign of Republican Daniel Templeton against Democratic incumbent Thomas Monaghan, and was at Penn Square in downtown Lancaster a day or two before the election. "We had a bus that was giving donuts and coffee to people," he recalls. Sid walked by and said, "Don't look so serious, your guy doesn't have a chance. Which he was right. He didn't have a chance." And in fact, Monaghan won, but only by 656 votes.

Wise's relationship with Tom Monaghan was especially meaningful for Judge Buckwalter because his brother-in-law, Dick Charles, "was Monaghan's campaign chairman. He and Sid were good buddies. That's primarily why I got involved with Sid, because Dick and I were brothers in law. Dick ran for Congress and I worked on Dick's campaign. I wasn't into politics much myself at that time. I was really outraged by the Bird machine [in Washington]. Bird was a Democrat who was just like Robert Byrd over in West Virginia, but this was another Bird. He had this overwhelming political machine which I really rebelled against. If I had any doubts of what party I was going to be in then, I picked the Republican. Then when I came back from Lancaster, it became very clear that – I was not political at that time. So I was a good student for Sid. I didn't have any particular politics at the time."

After graduating from F&M in 1958, Buckwalter went to the College of William and Mary School of Law and graduated in 1962. After graduation, he served as a legal aid attorney in Lancaster from 1964 to 1966, and then as a clerk to Judges John Bowman and Anthony Appel of the Court of Common Pleas in Lancaster County. He left that position to become an Assistant District Attorney in Lancaster County; he was named Lancaster County District Attorney in 1978. From 1980 to 1990, he served as a judge on the Court of Common Pleas of Lancaster County. In 1989, he was nominated by President George H.W. Bush to a seat on the U.S. District Court for the Eastern District of Pennsylvania and was approved in 1990 by the Senate.

Buckwalter stayed in touch with Professor Wise. "We would meet at alumni meetings and talk politics. All my life I've been Republican but that didn't matter. It

32

made more for fun and enjoyable conversations and stuff," Buckwalter noted. Plus, Professor Wise never cared about whether his students were Republicans or Democrats. "He didn't care, and he didn't cross lines at all in his lectures," said Buckwalter. "I never came out of [a class] even knowing Sid was a Democrat. I found that out later but I didn't know it at the time."

While there was not one moment or piece of advice that Buckwalter recalls, it was instead Professor Wise's energy that captivated him. "I would have to say that just his exuberance and excitement about politics. I just have these blips of Sid that are memorable and a strong feeling that you don't have toward every professor you ever had. That's what he brought out. I just remember being overwhelmed by his intellect. In later years I marveled at how Sid ever ended up at F&M, in a town that was really at that time small, totally different from his background and totally Republican. He knew that when he came on board. He knew what Franklin & Marshall was at that time and still came to Lancaster."

# John C. Pittenger – "Sid Wise Invented Networking"

John C. Pittenger wore many hats in his career. A summa cum laude graduate of Harvard College and cum laude graduate of Harvard Law School, he served as the Pennsylvania Secretary of Education, and was a State Representative from Lancaster. "Pitt," as he was known, died at age 79 in 2009; at the time, he was married to Pauline Leet. In addition, Pitt was a veteran, an educator, a farmer, a lawyer, and a law school dean, but he looked upon Sid Wise as a mentor and confidante. He was also a progressive, supporting the types of initiatives that were consistent with Sid Wise's ideals, including:

- Drafting the bill that set up the Pennsylvania Higher Education Assistance Agency scholarship program;

- Being a principal sponsor of the Mental Health/Mental Retardation Act of 1966;

- Developing reforms aimed at computerizing all state registration and election figures;

- Proposing graduated (or income-based) tuition at state colleges and universities;

- Being the first member of the General Assembly to bring high school seniors to Harrisburg on a regular basis to serve as pages in the House of Representatives;

- Serving as the Governor's Legislative Secretary and being instrumental in enacting legislation that (a) created Pennsylvania's state's first personal income tax bill, (b) reformed the Workers' Compensation and Unemployment Compensation Laws;

- Establishing due process rights for handicapped children;

- Creating the state government internship program for state college students; and,

- Leading the fight to mandate equal athletic programs for female students in public schools.

Pittenger was hired by a Lancaster law firm in 1958 but was quickly laid off because he was an active Democrat. Living near the F&M campus, he began attending social events and lectures at the College, where he met Sid Wise, Dick Schier and John Vanderzell, who were all Democrats. He also began teaching as an adjunct faculty member at F&M in 1961. Pittenger recalled that while Wise did not generally discuss his politics with his students, he was "a close advisor to [Lancaster] Mayor Monaghan[, who served from 1958-1962 and 1966-1974]. He was also very close to Senator Joseph Clark – a Democratic two term senator from Pennsylvania. So he knew everybody who was anybody in state democratic politics.

"As far as I'm concerned, [Sid Wise] invented networking." Pittenger said. "Any student could go in and see him and say, 'I want an internship this summer

35

in Harrisburg or Washington, or I want to meet somebody' or 'I want a recommendation for a law firm or a Ph.D. program' and Sidney was just marvelous at that. His rolodex must have been the best." "Sidney loved politics and he was just as willing to help republicans as democrats," said Pittenger, who noted that Wise was very close to Republican Congressman Ed Eshelman, who served for approximately ten years.

Pittenger also notes that Wise "was one of the four or five members of the faculty on whom [College President Keith Spalding] most depended to understand what the faculty was thinking, what their problems were, how he was viewed. He was the kind of person you would just go to and get good, honest advice about that sort of thing."

# John Buchanan – "You Can't Fool Me At All"

Considered one of the most influential theologians of his generation, John Buchanan, the former Pastor at the Fourth Presbyterian Church in Chicago, graduated from F&M in 1959, and received a master's degree in divinity from the University of Chicago's Divinity School/Theological Seminary in 1963, and an honorary Doctor of Humane Letters degree from F&M in 2002.

Buchanan spent the majority of his career as the Senior Pastor at Fourth Presbyterian Church in Chicago, and has been the editor/publisher of *The Christian Century* magazine since 1999. In addition, he was elected to be the Moderator (leader) of the Presbyterian Church (USA) for a one year term in 1996. In addition to authoring three books, Pastor Buchanan has authored numerous articles and delivered many sermons about tolerance, respect and acceptance of the practice of faith traditions outside Presbyterianism (Judaism, Islam, and Catholicism). He has spoken outwardly about accepting gay and lesbian members of the Church and endorses the idea that they should be allowed to be ordained ministers of the Presbyterian Church. In addition, he criticized those who stereotyped all Muslims as terrorists following the 9-11 attacks and he has openly diverged from the Christian "Right" in his views on politics and certain social issues, such as the inclusion of gays and lesbians as valued Christians.

But when thinking of persons whose influence made the most difference, Pastor Buchanan immediately recalls Sid Wise. In fact, in 2005 he authored an article in *The Christian Century*, entitled "Changing Lives. Great Teachers," in which he shared this anecdote:

> I loved reading in this issue about great teachers, teachers who have a way of changing lives. I found it impossible not to think about the teachers who changed me. My best college teacher was Sid Wise, professor of government at Franklin and Marshall College. He was short, funny, brilliant and engaging. I had done well in high school without exerting myself, something teachers always pointed out to my parents: "Doesn't work up to his potential." I wrote my first blue book exam for Professor Wise with breezy self-confidence. My life changed when the tests were returned. Wise wrote: "Mr. Buchanan: Lincoln said, 'You can fool all the people some of the time and some of the people all the time, but you can't fool me at all.' D- .

Buchanan did not shrink from the criticism. Instead, he recalls how Professor Wise captivated him and how he used the D- as a foundation for personal growth. "He was one of a kind. Government was one of the courses that I took as a freshman, "Introduction to [American Government]," and Sid Wise was the Professor," recalls Rev. Buchanan. "I just never heard an intellect on display like his; engaging, his rhetoric was compelling, and he was funny. I just loved listening to him talk. Obviously, I wasn't paying quite enough attention, but I found the experience enormously entertaining, and looked forward to it. Now I had had kind of a string of 12 years of uninterrupted success, applauded all the way along by the good people in Altoona, Pennsylvania. I had never seen a C in my life, let alone a D-minus. This came as a huge shock to me, and just kind of knocked my socks off. I mean, it was such a shock to my ego and to my psyche that I made an appointment with him and said, 'You must have made a mistake. I don't get D-minuses.' Anyhow, he was gentle but strong and tough, and he said, 'You didn't perform. You're not studying enough.' He had made that kind of half-insulting, tongue-in-cheek comment on the back page of the blue book. I believe I still have it."

From there, Buchanan grew as a student and as a person. "He was just very challenging, and he was kind, but not soapy, not soft. He said, 'You know, you're in college now and you've had a lifetime of success but you gotta pick up your game a little bit here – a lot,' The more I thought about it, the more I liked him, and thought, 'I like this subject, as a matter of fact.' I had no notion of what I wanted to do with my life at that point, and I was considering law school among other things until this."

"There was something that connected for me for the first time in my life, which ended in a career very different from politics, but in some ways were very connected. And it was Sid who brought the two together, the kind of academic pursuit of public life and public policy and how what you believe and what you're committed to needs to find some concrete expression in the public arena, whether it's in public institutions like the church or education or government. I credit Sid with that, and I credit my F&M Government/Sid Wise experience with pushing me off in that direction. Now, I suspect whatever vocation I would have chosen, I would have still been guided by that involvement, engagement, and put it out there."

"He had this gift of being able to discuss highly emotional, controversial issues, but with such lucidity and intelligence and sensitivity that he just encouraged thoughtfulness. And thoughtfulness is akin to civility when you're talking about the public conversation. Sid gave me a great gift in modeling how to talk about controversial issues with civility and sensitivity to the fact that not everybody in the room is on the same page on this issue. He modeled a dialogic way of teaching and thinking. I have found myself for 45 to 50 years engaged in heated stuff and always kind of in the middle, always trying to propose and trying to enable and facilitate dialog so that the ship doesn't sink while we're fighting about this."

"It's been the common theme in my vocation. I inserted myself into national Presbyterian politics 15 years ago and ran for Moderator of the General Assembly, the symbolic head of the Presbyterian Church. You travel around the world for a year and speak for the Church, but I did that right in the middle of probably the hottest time on the gay/lesbian issue, and found myself every single day for a year somewhere different in the country talking to people who were red-faced in anger or weeping in grief. It was the kind of thing that I saw Sid talking about and doing himself."

# Sanford Pinsker – Sid Was Mr. F&M

One of Sid Wise's long-time colleagues was Sanford ("Sandy") Pinsker, who taught English at F&M for 37 years. Dr. Pinsker, the Arthur and Katherine Shadek Professor of Humanities, Emeritus, and the author and editor of more than a dozen books, has published more than 800 articles, essays, editorials, and book reviews; he is generally considered *the* expert on Jewish American literature. Professor Pinsker and Dr. Wise "were good friends. Good friends from just about the time I hit campus. Sid wanted to read my dissertation on American Jewish literature and he actually read it. He liked it. We had lots to talk about, that and lots of other things."

As is common for Professor Pinsker, his perspective on events always is insightful, with a sprinkling of humor and sarcasm, qualities that made him so popular on campus. "Sid famously described F&M in the days when it was known as a small Christian college, as one that did not necessarily have a Kosher kitchen," Pinsker recalls. "That was Sid's definition. Sid once walked in on the first day of a Government class and said, 'There at least a dozen people who know more about American Government than I do; none of them is in this room.'"

But Sid's warmth showed through. "In one word, Sid was a 'Mensch' in every sense of that Yiddish word. He was kind. He was funny. He was principled. He was a liberal back in the days when that was not a bad word. He was Mr. F&M. For years that's how he was known, as Mr. F&M. There's nobody that exemplified the best of the College more than Sid."

"He could obviously enjoy students no matter what their particular bent was in terms of politics," Pinsker recalls. "That didn't matter. The Government Department in those days prided itself on the fact that you wouldn't know where their politics were. They didn't announce it or wear it on their sleeves. I mean, after a while I'm sure you figured out that Sid was a Democrat, but for a lot of the kids in the class that never came up. You don't break out of your character as a Gov Professor to start talking about what your personal politics are. Sid just never did that – it's like Hamlet breaking out to tell you he was born in New Jersey. This kid is playing Hamlet. You don't do that. You don't break out of your character as a Gov Professor to start talking about what your personal politics are, but I think that's what people do now all the time, and that's a shame, but there it is."

When asked to recall any particular stories about Sid Wise, Pinsker immediately mentioned the numerous protests that permeated the campus during the Vietnam War, and the "protest tree" that was the symbol of the movement. "During the Vietnam War, the protest tree was filled every day with anti-war sentiment," Pinsker explains. "Then, after the war was over, it devolved as it were, at least according to one student, into a place to sell stereo equipment, a place to advertise things. The tree was not for protest anymore. So, one morning, a kid had taken a lot of time to write a long screed that scrolled down the entire length of the tree. What it said was, keep this tree clear for protest. During the Vietnam War we protested the war and now we have to make sure that it stays true to that heritage.

"It went all the way down – the kid must have worked for hours. Right at the bottom, about eye length, somebody had written, "Need Ride to Allentown." I thought that was so funny. I cracked up. Then, while having lunch in the faculty dining room that afternoon, I said, 'You know, if I could find that kid, I could teach that kid how to write because that kid's got it.' Sid looked up sheepishly and said, 'That was me who wrote it.' I said, 'Take my class! I mean, I don't care.' Sid said, 'No I heard you're too hard a grader.' Sid had this wonderful sense of understated dry humor."

"That was just wonderful. And, 'Need Ride to Allentown' said everything to diffuse that kid's self-righteous screaming, which Sid couldn't stand because he couldn't stand people that were self-righteous. We had plenty of them then. I'm sure there's plenty of them now. Students and faculty alike, but that was never Sid."

Professor Pinsker also noted how Sid's influence impacted a former student. "Kenny Duberstein was on the Charlie Rose Show and he mentioned this unremarkable fact, which has now become remarkable, that politics is the art of compromise. Well, Kenny got that certainly from Sid who understood what compromise was about and how you craft a compromise. That's what Kenny did as Chief of Staff [to President Reagan] and ended up to be one of the most highly regarded Chiefs of Staff in our time. But people have lost, certainly now, any sense of compromise on either side of the aisle."

Describing Sid's influence on the College as well, Pinsker said. "I wasn't teaching at the college when the Board of Trustees forced President Bowman to leave, but the aftermath of that has ensured us to this day that the Professional Standards Committee is a Professional Standards Committee of elected faculty members and we're not beholden to a college president or a narrow group of trustees. That's not how you decide who gets tenure. But that's how they used to decide who got tenure. The idea that you could pursue ideas wherever they would take you is what makes a liberal education a liberal education. You can't pursue ideas and stop if it's going to offend somebody.

"That's one of the problems with these names on buildings. The person who puts up the building thinks that he or she calls the tune, but that's not so. The person bought the bricks, and inside the walls people are free to pursue ideas. And they are often very unhappy people, these donors, but that's too bad. Either you're for the liberal arts or you aren't. F&M has a nice tradition of being in the liberal arts. It's still there and Sid is one of the people that made that possible. He's got a long stake in the place."

# H. William Gray – "Never Hire Interns"

To many people, the name Bill Gray is synonymous with the United Negro College Fund. To some, it signifies one of the highest ranking African Americans in the history of Congress. To others, it represents the story of how a seemingly random contact with a teacher can change not only one individual's life, but also the country's direction.

The first hint of where Bill Gray's career might lead appeared in the March 13, 1963 issue of the Franklin and Marshall College *Student Weekly*, entitled "Gray, Lasky Get Internships in Congress, Journalism:"

> W. Herbert Gray, Class of '63 has received a political internship through the Pennsylvania Center for Education in Politics (P.C.E.P.) to serve under Democratic Congressman Nix of Philadelphia.
> Dr. Sidney Wise, of the government department is the chairman of P.C.E.P. ...
> Gray is a pre-theology history major. He is a dormitory counselor, a member of the Sociology Club, History Club, Phi Upsilon Kappa Pre-Theology Fraternity, Committee for Social Action and the varsity basketball, track and football teams.
> Gray is affiliated with the Democratic Party. His father, William Herbert Gray, Jr., minister at the Bright Hope Baptist Church in Philadelphia, is also active in the Democratic Party. He

served as a campaign manager for Richardson Dilworth in the 1962 gubernatorial election for the Philadelphia area.

Gray, who passed away in 2013, was not a typical political science major at F&M. In fact, he never took a course in government while at the college. Rather, when he arrived at F&M in the fall of 1958, he expected that he would follow in his father's footsteps after graduation from the then all-male college. Gray, who was known at the time as Herb, had anticipated attending the seminary and embarking on a career as a "teacher and a preacher." What he did not know is that Government Professor Sid Wise had noticed him and had other thoughts about a possible career for the young man.

Wise approached Gray just weeks before graduation. "After the Gettysburg basketball game at Franklin and Marshall, 1963, I was a senior, and at that game we upset Gettysburg. Sid came up to me after the game was over and he said, 'Mr. Gray?' and I said, 'Yes, Dr. Wise?' Everybody knew who Sid Wise was. He said, 'I would like to talk to you.' And I said 'yes.' He said, "I want you to come by my office and so we can talk. Have you ever thought about getting into public policy?" I said 'no.' He said, 'Well, I've watched, you've got leadership qualities. I want to talk to you.'"

"When a professor like Sid Wise says I want to see you, you go see him even if he's not your professor. I called up, made an appointment, went by, and that's when he said, 'I would like to arrange for you to become an intern for a program that I direct in Washington so that you can be introduced into public service, and maybe one time in your life you might consider it. I've been watching you even though I've never been one of your professors and you've never taken any courses in the Government Department or Political Science. You really show leadership skills, and people in public policy need a hand. Maybe you ought to have an introduction. I have an internship program that I'd like to recommend you for.' And he got me the internship that summer in Washington, D.C. The conversation lasted about five minutes at best, maybe even less. In two more months, I'm graduating. I was a History major, and I didn't have any more courses to take."

Gray graduated, but not before accepting the internship proposal. He recalls that "It was very unusual in many ways in that most of the people who got those internships were Government majors or Political Science majors. Secondly, they usually came between their junior and senior year." After completing his internship, Gray obtained a master's degree in divinity from Drew Theological Seminary in 1966 and a master's degree in Church history from the Princeton Theological Seminary in 1970, after which he served as a faculty member and professor of religion at various colleges and universities.

In 1976, the 33 year old Gray, who became the pastor at Philadelphia's Bright Hope Baptist Church (his father's church), decided to run for office. "At 25, I had reached my dream to be a minister and a teacher, a preacher teacher. I had it, and I was in a wonderful time. I never had any intention of running for public office when I went to Philadelphia. I started getting involved in the community life and found myself speaking out on the issues that were public-policy issues, but at the same time, being a minister of the church," Gray recalls.

47

"People said, well why don't you get into office? So I finally said, okay I'll run, and I ran for Congress just to see if I could run a good race, maybe hit 30 percent of the vote. As it turned out I got 49.9 percent of the vote [in 1976] with no budget, no money, talking about leadership issues centered around Philadelphia, political issues that would not only lead into Congress but also lead at home in a new political direction."

"The Democratic Party was controlled then by Frank Rizzo, so I was talking about how we need to change that whole direction in the Democratic Party. That's how I got into politics, and it was an extension of my role as a minister, an advocate for human issues and concerns in a very repressive political environment in Philadelphia at that time. So we built a new coalition that became the dominant force in Philadelphia, and eventually led to the election of Wilson Goode, Eddie Rendell, John Street, and the old-style political organization of the Rizzo years was swept away." In 1978, two years after losing the primary by 339 votes, Gray defeated Congressman Nix in the primary and was easily elected in the November election. After winning the primary, Gray received a congratulatory note from Professor Wise, "Sid said, 'Be careful taking interns. You can have interns, but don't hire any from Franklin & Marshall.'"

Gray's rise in Congress was meteoric. Gray was elected by the 42 freshman Democrats as their representative to the Steering and Policy Committee and represented the freshmen on the Democratic Leadership Committee. He was also appointed to the House Budget Committee and the Foreign Affairs Committee, and was the secretary of the Congressional Black Caucus. "I was the first African-American to chair the Budget Committee," Gray explains. "Also, I was the youngest member of Congress ever to chair the Budget Committee; the youngest in age, as well as youngest in time served. I'd only been in Congress six years when I was elected. I became the first Black ever to be chairman of the Democratic Caucus, and then I became the majority WHIP, the first black there."

One of the key moments of his Congressional career came when he received a note from Sid Wise, explaining that Ken Duberstein was White House Chief of Staff. "I did not know Ken when I was at Franklin Marshall," Gray says. "Sid sent me a note saying there's another F&M guy, he's on the other side. You guys really ought to get together and get to know each other, and we did, and we've been friends ever since." Not only were they friends, they accomplished a lot by working together.

"One of the things Sid tried to point out, at least for me, is you can violently, strongly disagree with another person's point of view on a public policy issue, but you should never condemn them to being subhuman immoral characters because they differ from you. One thing I remember from Sid is that stability is the cement that holds the bricks of democracy together," Gray recalls.

"I think one of the tragedies that has occurred in American public policy debate in the last 15, 20 years is this lack of stability where politicians and their followers make the other people out as less than human beings or real evil, they're the Dark Side, and that makes it very difficult for you to reach a consensus, compromise, and to move the nation forward. If you haven't condemned them to the trash heap of decadent humanity, then you've recognized that maybe something they say may have value, and it may slightly alter your viewpoint a little bit, but you listen. You listen to the opposition," he notes.

Gray capitalized on his work on the Budget Committee and was selected as chairman of the committee, replacing Congressman Richard Gephardt. Gray also drafted the party platform for the 1988 Democratic Convention, uniting a broad coalition of Democrats under a platform of "that which uniquely binds us together as Democrats." Gray was next chosen as the first African-American chairman of the House Democratic Caucus. Following his selection, Gray noted that the position called for building coalitions, "I hope we can tie our ropes together so we can be one party and show the nation what we stand for as Democrats," Gray stated. A few months later, Gray was chosen as House Majority Whip, the third-ranking leadership position. At the time, Gray was the highest-ranking African American in Congressional history.

Of course, there were those who remained skeptical of the ascent of an African American. "I remember when I was elected," Gray recalled. "I was doing a national television show with two black journalists. I was vice-chair of the Black Caucus. I was on the Budget Committee and the Appropriations Committee, and they asked me in the interview, 'What are your plans Congressman for the next session?'" I said, 'I'm thinking about running for Budget Committee Chairman," he recalls. "The two of them broke out laughing on national television. Not smiling, laughing, and they said, 'Are you serious?' And I said, 'yes.' That December I won, and nobody thought that a Black could be responsible for the macroeconomic policy of the whole country."

Throughout his tenure in Congress, Gray stayed in touch with Professor Wise. "Sid would see I was doing something, and he'd write me a note and give me his point of view, or he would share another point of view," Gray recalls. "He would just simply say, 'I saw you on television on *Meet the Press*. You did a great job, but let me suggest in the future – look at this. Always very positive, always very helpful. Sid made me very proud that a professor at the institution where you went still cared about your growth and development to make observations and make suggestions. A professor who you respected is still looking at you, still watching you, still interested in your development. I mean that's a real compliment."

Gray surprised many by resigning from Congress in 1991; in doing so, he agreed to head the United Negro College Fund. Gray served as President and CEO of the College Fund until March 2004. In 1999, Microsoft Chairman Bill Gates asked Gray what could be done to help increase the number of students of color who graduate from college. As a result of that conversation, Gates agreed to create the Gates Millennium Scholars (GMS) program, which annually selects 1,000 talented students to receive a "good-through-graduation" scholarship to use at any college or university. In addition to funding a student's college education, the program provides mentoring services for academic and personal development. It also offers an online resource center that provides internship, fellowship and scholarship information.

In 1994, President Clinton asked Gray to serve as his special adviser on Haiti, which was then embroiled in civil war. Gray's efforts to restore democracy to the island nation won him a Medal of Honor from Haitian President Jean-Bertrand Aristide.

More recently, Gray took pride in the election of Barrack Obama, and pondered how Professor Wise would view the election. "I think Sid would be quite happy, and I think he would be astonished, but I think he would also be quite happy because it would mean a maturing of the political process, overcoming an awful racial history in this country and a period in American history that we don't even like to talk about – and we certainly don't tell the truth about – which is slavery – a period that really only ended in the 60s," he says.

"Sid would say 'God, in 35 years we've come to the point where we can overcome our past, our history and our ugliness and elect a black guy.' So I think he would truly be amazed. He would be pleased, and he would say this is the kind of America that we really need to achieve. It's where it is the competency of the character and not the color of the skin. And we're just moving a little bit closer to that," Gray notes.

No matter where his career took him, Gray thought back on the advice and counsel he received from Sid Wise. "Sid was just an extraordinary individual, very impressive," he said. "I'd never had him for a course, but he was well-known, well-liked throughout the campus and well respected by everybody, not just his students but those like myself who had never been a student of his but knew him to be fair, a person of great character and great ability. When I did leave Franklin & Marshall and did get into public service as a

Congressman, from time to time he would drop me these notes, and they would be like, 'Remember: don't hire any interns.' And I've thrown him a note back saying, 'Yeah, especially from Franklin & Marshall.'"

# Pauline Leet – She Defined "Sexist"

> When you argue...that since fewer women write good poetry this justifies their total exclusion, you are taking a position analogous to that of the racist – I might call you in this case a "sexist"... Both the racist and the sexist are acting as if all that has happened had never happened, and both of them are making decisions and coming to conclusions about someone's value by referring to factors which are in both cases irrelevant.[2]

Pauline Leet's claim to fame will always be that she coined the word "sexist," but the story behind the "word" and her relationship with Sid Wise are far more telling. She arrived at F&M in 1963 with her first husband, who was hired to teach in the English Department. When the English Department faculty suffered two sudden deaths, Roger Rowland, the interim department chair "gathered together a bunch of faculty wives," including Pauline Leet, to teach freshman composition. The wives, who "became Roger Rowland's Irregulars," found themselves unemployed after that semester.

For Pauline Leet, however, it was merely the first of countless positions she would hold at the College, where she claims to have had virtually every job "except a Presidency and buildings and grounds."

---

[2] "Student-Faculty Forum," Franklin and Marshall College, from the paper, "Women and the Undergraduate," by Pauline M. Leet, November 18, 1965.

Leet met Sid Wise "almost immediately" upon arriving Lancaster, and became close friends with Sid's wife Eileen. "But Sid and I were very close." Because of her many roles, Leet finds it difficult to differentiate between those times when she "dropped by for coffee in the kitchen with Eileen, and staying on after Sidney got home to discuss what was going on at the college. He was just a lovely, complete 360 degree human being. I remember some of his expressions when he was going to tell you something confidential, which really wasn't very confidential, and he'd say, *d'entre nous*."

But the word "sexist" remains a defining moment. In 1965, the College had a "Student Faculty Forum,[during which Bob Mezzie, a visiting faculty member] used his address in the Forum in October of '65, to say that he advised students to burn their draft cards; naturally, this was picked up by the Lancaster *New Era*, and it was a brouhaha." Leet, who was then Director of Special Programs, recalls being viewed "around campus as a fairly outspoken person."

"So the kids asked me if I could give one, because they were so thrilled and wanted another rousing act to follow the Bob Mezzie thing. So I gave them a sexy title, "Women and the Undergraduate," because, you remember at that time, we were all male. The buses would pull up on the weekend from the girls' colleges, it was a meat market, it was really disgusting. So, I wrote the whole thing out, and what I said was: 'The reason that I've been asked to speak to you is because I am a specialist in the disadvantaged, and as students at an all-male school, you are among the disadvantaged.' And then I went on to talk about how no women were studied in English literature, da da da da. And then, I said: 'You might call this a sexist thing.' And that was, apparently, the first time that it was used."

In 1969, Leet was at Harvard, but when the Trustees were meeting to consider going co-ed, students contacted and asked her to "come back and join them in a march outside the hall where the trustees were meeting. I said, I really couldn't do that, but I would send them a telegram, and the telegram that I sent said, "Remember what I always say: 'Without girls, *Peter Pan* is *Lord of the Flies*.'" So that was read.

Of course, Sid Wise was instrumental in the decision to admit women to F&M. "I don't think anything happened without people consulting Sid. His office door was always open." Leet also recalls when the college offered a team-taught course called "The Black Experience," and disgruntled students took Professor Wise and other profs hostage to protest grades they believed were unfair. "It was a jointly-taught course; but when the students found that they were actually going to be graded, they erupted, the grounds being that they provided the black experience and the teacher just came in and heard about it. I think that was an extremely traumatic experience for Sid. I think it took him more than a year or two to come to terms with that. You know, the relationship between students and faculty was kind of a two-way relationship: You have a faculty member like Sid who gives everything he has to the kids, and actually for the rest of their lives; the reciprocity is that the kids pay attention and work hard and do good, and so forth. Some of the black students really used the occasion to let out so many things that had upset them and pissed them off, not just at F&M, but in their life."

It's funny, the Class of '71 invited me to be one of the former faculty members to come to their reunion, and among the guests was one of the leaders of the rebellion. All he wanted to talk about was how I drove him to his student teaching job, and that my car was such terrible shape that he had to hold the door handle to keep it from opening. I would have thought [he might have talked about the incident], but he became a faculty member and he's a dean of a law school now. I don't think any of those guys had any idea what it did to the faculty."

# Kenneth Duberstein – "You Guys Need To Be Talking – Listen To One Another"

Ken Duberstein has been called "The Fixer" and one of Washington's "pre-eminent wise men"[3] for his ability to know whom to contact and which buttons to push in almost any situation. But Ken Duberstein was not always such a sage; like any other "insider," it took years for him to learn, develop and hone the skills necessary to become one of the go-to people in Washington for both Republicans and Democrats. What most people do not know is that Duberstein traces much of his growth to his years in Lancaster and to the advice he received in college – and for decades after – from Sid Wise.

Duberstein candidly admits that when he was in the White House as Reagan's Chief of Staff, and needed advice about how to handle a crisis, or how to manage the many personalities he encountered, he would call upon his college professor and mentor, Sid Wise, for confidential advice. The fact that he trusted his professor, and knew that their conversations would not end up on the front page of *The New York Times* was critical to his ability to help President Reagan and others govern effectively.

When he arrived in Lancaster from Brooklyn in 1961 as a raw freshman, Duberstein had no idea what his future would hold. "I went to F&M not knowing what I was going to major in. F&M was known then as a big pre-med school," Duberstein says. "I took either biology

---

[3] *Pennsylvania Avenue*, p. 23

or chemistry at 8 a.m. on a Monday morning and said to myself, 'I'm not going to be a doctor.'"

Duberstein enrolled in his first Government course during his sophomore year, and it opened his eyes. "My first course was not with Sid Wise. It was with Dick Schier," he recalls. "Dick Schier started off the class by saying, 'Some people say the masses are asses, and this whole semester we're going to prove why the masses are usually right.' And I said, oh my God, somebody I can understand."

At that point, Duberstein's perspective changed. "I started going to the Government Club meetings and hanging around the Government office. One of the people whom I started interacting with was Sid, whom I only took two classes with. But I used to go to his house for dinner. I got involved with everything. I remember he took a semester off, a sabbatical, to work for Senator Joe Clark. I thought that was really neat. Here was a professor – as Dick Schier was and John Vanderzell was – who not only understood the theory, but also understood the practice of politics, the art of governing. That it wasn't just Socrates and Plato and Aristotle or comparative government organization. But Sid actually got his hands dirty and got involved. So I said, my God, this is something I want to do too. I became president of the Government Club, all my good grades were in Government. I really got inspired by him."

Duberstein graduated F&M in 1965, and received an internship with second-term New York Senator Jacob Javits, who was considered a liberal. But Duberstein ran into a most basic problem, he did not have the money to pay for housing at his new position. "Sid said, 'don't worry about it, I think I can find some money for you,'" and obtained a $500 stipend from the Pennsylvania Center for Education and Politics to cover Duberstein's living expenses.

There was a catch. "Sid said to me, 'I will help you get this thing, but you have to promise to come back and help others.' And all of a sudden I started meeting other F&M graduates with a willingness to help out."

Meanwhile, as his career developed, Duberstein sought advice. "And who did I go to for quiet advice? Sid, and Dick and John, but especially Sid. The person who could help me understand all the cross-currents was Sid Wise. It wasn't just about governance, it was about where all the booby traps lie, where the opportunities were," he recalls. "This was politics. It was the art of governing. Sid always followed my career, and always would stay in touch. A phone call, a note, this was before emails. I hired some F&M interns, including David Wise [Sid's son]."

Duberstein returned to F&M in the late 1960s to work as an administrative assistant to the President of the College, Keith Spalding. In 1970, he accepted a position with the General Services Administration and became the Director of Congressional and Intergovernmental Affairs. Six years later, he became the Deputy Undersecretary of Labor for Legislative and Intergovernmental Activities for the Gerald Ford administration. He continued to build his career in government as the Assistant and the Deputy Assistant to the President for Legislative Affairs from 1981 to 1983. Before becoming part of the Reagan administration, he was Vice President and Director of Business-Government Relations of the Committee for Economic Development, and Vice President of Timmons

& Company Inc., a lobbying firm. Duberstein eventually joined the Reagan administration in 1987 as Deputy Chief of Staff and was appointed White House Chief of Staff in 1988. He was awarded the President's Citizens Medal by President Reagan in January 1989.

But in the White House, Duberstein had one safety net he could always rely upon – Sid Wise. "When I was in the White House, I would call him periodically when I needed some advice from someone not inside the Beltway. He would say, 'Now, you're the professor, and I'm the student,'" he recalls, noting that Wise's advice was always helpful and practical. "When you're in the White House, not just for a president, but if you're in a senior position there, people don't always tell you straight. It's a very private existence, because most people when they talk to you, want something. What's the President's position going to be on this? What's the administration going to do on that? I found to keep myself grounded I would pick up the phone and talk to some of my friends back in Lancaster, headlined, number one, by Sid. How is this playing in Lancaster County? Does this make sense to you? What am I missing? What do you think we should be doing? Do we have this calibrated right? And it could be anywhere from defense spending to taking on Tip O'Neil on something or a tax bill. Are we being too firm? Should we show a little bit of willingness to compromise here? Is this a dead end? From your vantage point at Franklin and Marshall, from your years observing the system – I knew (A), he would tell me straight, and (B), it would stop with him. I could trust him. It wasn't going to be in the front page of the *New York Times*, the *Wall Street Journal*, or the *Lancaster New Era* the same day."

One situation Duberstein remembers involved a Republican Senator who could not be convinced to support one of President Reagan's policies. "I remember being very frustrated trying to figure out a certain senator we couldn't convince to vote our way, a Republican, big Republican, on a defense spending issue. Cap Weinberger wanted 13 percent, the Senator was willing to give us 3 percent, and we knew that 7 percent was the answer, and he wouldn't go there. I remember calling Sid one evening, [saying] 'I can't figure this out, I've talked to the senator, the President's talked to the senator.' And I remember Sid chuckling on the phone and saying, *'What you're missing is that the senator votes first for his home state, second for the institution of the senate, and third, if those two don't matter and the president is of his own party, he'll consider giving them a vote.'* All the lights went on. He was voting for his constituents back home, what he thought was helpful to them. Where are you going to get that advice in Washington?"

Ronald Reagan's ability to work with Republicans and Democrats was a natural fit for Duberstein, whose career has also bridged the parties. He is widely viewed as one of the people who created the coalitions that allowed Reagan to fulfill his agenda. "I am viewed, I think, as somebody – almost a dying breed in Washington – who can reach across both sides. I have a lot of relationships in the middle, left, right, but not far left and not far right. I've always been acknowledged as someone who's interested in governing. I learned some of that from Sid Wise. I certainly learned a lot of that from Ronald Reagan, an old Democrat. My job under Reagan in the beginning was to put together the bipartisan coalition against Tip

O'Neil. I had to be the person in the White House who sometimes is arguing if we're going to put up the Democratic votes we need because we didn't have a majority in the house, we had to. Reagan understood. It was the art of governing."

One of the reasons for Duberstein's success in the White House was his relationship with fellow F&M alumnus Bill Gray, who was then an up-and-coming Congressman. However, the two men did not know each other, until they heard from Sid, who sent them each notes, urging them to meet.

Duberstein recalls the letter about Bill Gray. It said, "*You guys have a different philosophy, but you need to talk public policy with a result.*" The two men met, and a lifetime friendship was created. "Bill was in a position of authority in the Congress, in the House. I was in a position of some authority in the White House. We were listening to one another. We talked to one another. I didn't expect Bill Gray to vote for what Ronald Reagan wanted on very many things, but he'd share information with me, and I shared our point of view with him. As a result, there was better public policy. Sometimes we won. A few times he won. But there wasn't the acrimony and the brickbats, and the fighting that there really is now. We would talk to one another. It is not something that ever got publicized. This was not something that would wind up in the *Washington Post* the next day, or on the network news. But that's what governing is all about, understanding one another and seeing, can you find common ground? That's civilized."

"I was doing stuff in the White House on the African development bank, because Bill Gray told me that it made sense. And I looked at it and I said, he's right," Duberstein remembers. "Where did it come from? It came from Sid Wise. Not the bank, but the relationship. *You guys need to be talking – listen to one another.* One of the things that I found interesting about the Obama campaign was that Obama, like Ronald Reagan, would say, what's the harm in listening to the opponent? *You got to listen to what your adversary wants. You don't always have to agree with him. You're not negotiating, you're understanding one another.* That was Sid Wise."

After leaving the White House, Duberstein's influence has grown, and he devotes his efforts to a wide range of causes. He is Vice Chairman of the Kennedy Center for Performing Arts, on the Board of Directors of Fannie Mae, and an active trustee of both F&M and Johns Hopkins University. In 1989, he created the Duberstein Group, a strategic planning and consulting firm in Washington D.C., where he currently lives with his family. Duberstein's career continues to be involved in significant political events.

The election of Barrack Obama was also a defining moment in Duberstein's career, because he endorsed the Democrat, not his party's nominee. "What I saw in this last election with the nominees, was Obama looking very much to the future, and speaking about hope. I became very comfortable with the idea that while I may not agree with Obama on everything, I thought instinctively he was the right person and the steady person that we needed in America after eight years of very tough fighting with George Bush. I think Sid would have been very dismayed with how the Bush years turned out. I think he would have seen Obama as a transformational candidate and possibly a transformational president. I think Sid would have been concerned whether or not he had enough experience with foreign and domestic policies," Duberstein noted.

Duberstein and Bill Gray regularly attended events at which they discussed political events, but always note that they were introduced to each other through the note of a dear professor who believed they could learn and benefit from knowing one another. That was the wisdom of Sidney Wise.

Duberstein recalls: "He was a rare teacher, who talked about the day-in, day-out process of governing, putting coalitions together, making government work." Duberstein's reflection on Sid's influence in his life and career echoes how incredibly insightful and passionate Sid was about politics. But mostly, Wise helped Duberstein learn about "The Art of Governing."

"It's the art of the possible, it's how much you can do," Duberstein explained. "Sid always talked to us about [how] we're really a nation of incrementalists. We're not a nation that takes things in big chunks. You march the ball down the field. That's why I like going to the football games at F&M, you see them work down the field. And we learned that's the way you govern too. I remember talking with Sid after the Moscow Summit, and after the summit here in Washington. I remember talking to him when big international events would take place. He influenced my politics in the sense of I don't like Don Quixote missions. I understand public service is a high calling and I really treasure that. Sid Wise always said, 'Do the right thing. Do what you think is right, not what's political. The best politics is good governing.' That's what Sid said. You take care of the little things and the big things kind of take care of themselves."

# George Harad – "You Don't Know Everything And You'll Never Know Everything"

Not every Government major at F&M went on to public service. For example, George Harad graduated magna cum laude in 1965 and then received a Master of Arts degree from Harvard University in 1970 and an MBA from Harvard in 1971. He was also a George F. Baker Scholar, which is the highest honor awarded to a Harvard student before graduation. Following his graduation from Harvard, Harad became a successful businessman, joining Boise Cascade Corporation in 1971. The company changed its name to OfficeMax; Harad would eventually become Chairman of the Board of Directors and Chief Executive Officer of Office Max in 1995, serving until 2005, when he retired and formed Harad Capital Management.

Harad's roots were more humble. He was the first and only person in his family to go to college. He applied to F&M, which gave him a scholarship and "some job opportunities that allowed [him] to be able to afford the place."

Knowing that he did not want to be a doctor or scientist, Harad considered majoring in either English or Government, but selected Government because he "was more interested in government and public policy." During his time at F&M, he got to know the Big Three, Professors Schier, Vanderzell and Wise, recalling in particular one survey course he took – and whose final he misunderstood. "In fact, I got to know them quite well because there was a survey course that was taught at the time. It actually ran two semesters and at the end of the second semester, there was a final exam and I remember this very, very clearly. One of the questions was to describe the political events in France after 1789. I misread the question and wrote a very good essay I might say, on the decade in France after 1799; which I think threw them all for a loop. So I got to know them quite well as we all discussed what the hell to do with this eight page answer."

It was the little things that Professor Wise did that made the biggest difference. "Sid actually helped me in a couple of other ways since I was constantly broke," Harad recalls. "He got me a job as the ticket collector at the Green Room. I also worked part time in the Government Department office as well as working for the library, which is a job the school gave me. On at least a couple of occasions, I actually babysat for his children. I think without trying to be very overt about it, he was trying to help me out and make sure I had enough money to eat.'

Even after graduating from F&M, Professor Wise was there to help, and his F&M background made a difference once Harad decided not to be an academic. "As my business career progressed, I had two advantages. I knew how to be an academic, so I knew how to get the information I needed and assemble it into a coherent form in order to act on it as a business person," he says. "The second is I've had a continuing respect for the work that academics do, so a number of the academics who taught at Harvard Business School have written and have helped in different ways over the years."

"I think Sid's impact was less what was taught than the behavior of the individuals themselves. The professors were very accessible, willing to debate issues, even when you were on opposite sides and very respectful of their students, which is something that I've tried to carry forward with people working for me. You don't know everything and you'll never know everything, and the people who work with you and for you can always contribute to what you've learned and what the enterprise is doing. That was just an attitude Sid had."

# Al Zuck – "The Bureaucrat Everyone Trusted"

When people think of bureaucrats, they tend to picture people who perform their duties robotically, with no consideration for the public whom they serve. In reality, bureaucrats help assure that government does what it is supposed to, in the way it was intended to do. Alfred M. Zuck, a 1957 graduate of F&M, embodies the bureaucrat who not only does his job, but also makes government work more efficiently and more effectively. Mr. Zuck is the recipient of the Presidential Distinguished Executive Rank Award (1980); the Distinguished Career Service Award (1974); and the William A. Jump Memorial Award (1974). He received a master's degree from the Maxwell School of Syracuse University in public administration in 1958.

It all began at F&M, and his matriculation at the school was mere happenstance. "I had TB and my doctor felt that it would probably be better if I went locally and lived at home. So that's why I came to F&M. I commuted my first year. But after that, I lived in a fraternity." In fact, Zuck believes he "probably would have been a doctor if he hadn't gotten involved with the Government Department. [But he had a] natural sense of politics."

While a freshman, he decided to enroll in the American government class. "Until I actually got into the class, I never met any of the professors. Never met Sid at all. Here I was, coming out of a little high school, going to college, and being in a totally new environment. Here is this country bumpkin kid, and one of the first things I remember about Sid, I had never seen this before. Sid always carried a cloth book bag over his shoulder, a red cloth book bag. That was kind of a singular identifying moment for me with Sid. I'd never seen that any place and there was never any other professor around that did that. I think it's a Harvard tradition or something."

Although he was a government major, Zuck was not particularly interested in politics and political parties. He "was into the administration stuff. When I was [at F&M], there were no courses on bureaucracy. The stuff I really liked was Constitutional Law and Political Theory. [Meanwhile,] Sid really was twisting my arm to do an honors thesis. As I was thinking about that. [Wise, Schier and Vanderzell] were really trying to get some attention to the department, and they wanted to be able to be in the commencement program and show their colleagues that they had somebody doing an honors thesis and stuff. But I think Sid also was trying, really wanted me to go the academic route."

Wise also transformed Zuck's political views. "As a kid growing up," he remembers, "my dad was politically active. He was involved in getting a borough charter for the town and I can remember the 1940 elections, collecting Wilkie literature and stuff. I mean, we were a great Republican family. I was a Republican until I got some education, and Sid was really that vehicle. I mean I took that first course and basically all of those guys were not theoretical. They were applied. It was the McCarthy era, the hearings, and I mean, there were a lot of nasty things going on.'

"While I was a student [at F&M], I used to ride with Ed Eshelman , the State representative who later became a Congressman and represented the District that Lancaster's in for quite a long time. But it was really the exposure to Sid, and my natural inclination, and interest in these kinds of things. I was really hooked at that point."

Wise helped Zuck get a job as a page in Harrisburg. He also recalls that when he graduated "there were only seven or six or eight of us who were [government] majors. But at least half of them were avid Republicans. The capacity that Sid had to be respected, loved by people who disagreed with him politically. It was really very, very incredible. Sid had a great demeanor about him. He was easy to deal with, made you feel very comfortable. He wasn't bombastic. He wasn't screaming at students."

Zuck is perhaps most remembered for two events. In 1983, President Ronald Reagan appointed him Acting Assistant Administrator of the Environmental Protection Agency, succeeding John P. Horton, who resigned at the request of the White House amid complaints that the agency was poorly managed and not performing its core functions well. Zuck recalls that the White House was "trying to strategize about how to make a clean sweep in EPA. A number of the top officials had left for a variety of reasons, conflicts and others. So it was decided [that they would] send in new people for legislative affairs, Superfund Management, and Inspector General. In the conversations – the OMB director apparently said, 'Al Zuck's the guy [for EPA]. He's got great rapport with Republican members of Congress and – Congressional relations was one of the problems.' [In addition, Ken] Duberstein was there."

Zuck recalls the events leading up to the appointment. "I got a call from the Cabinet Secretary – at 4:00 one afternoon saying, 'Hey Al, the President is reassigning you to be the Acting Associate Administrator in the EPA, and you're to report there tomorrow morning.' And I said, 'Hey. Geez, I got no interest in this. I'm leaving government in July. I had already had my fill of it after 25 years." He was told to "appear at the EPA Administrative Offices at 9:00 in the morning [the next day, and was] told that three other people were [joining him]. We were to meet with [Anne] Burford. She was not present. We were told we would meet with her later. Then we were told that there was a press conference at 4:00 at which she was going to meet the new staff – introduce the staff to the press and make it public."

"At 1:00 I get a call to go to Burford's office, and I thought this was the meeting. As it turns out, I was the only one. She said, 'I don't know you. I don't want you. I don't need you. I'm a born manager. But the White House has sent you here. So you go and occupy the chair.' And I don't know what in the hell caused me to respond. I said, 'if you think I was sent here to babysit this organization, you're mistaken.' Well, all hell broke loose. She's screaming and crying, 'I'm going to see the President,' and storms out of the room. I thought, great. I'm back at Labor – and this was in February."

"My plans were to leave in July 1983, and it's 'great, I'm back at Labor.' I didn't hear anything. Four o'clock came, so I'm on my way to the press conference. The press release was all issued and everything. I happened to pass Burford in the hall, and she said that there's no need for you to come. I said fine. I went home. I got a call that evening from Craig Fuller. He was a Cabinet secretary. He said, 'Al, what the hell happened?' I said 'Burford and I had a session and she's not really interested in having me and I didn't want to go in the first place, so I'll just stay at Labor.' He said, 'no, no, no, no, no. We've got bigger fish to fry. Just hang in there. As a matter of fact, the President's leaving tomorrow. He has to host the Queen – the Queen of England, Queen Elizabeth – on the Queen Mary out in Long Beach. I'm going to be calling in 4:00 every afternoon, and I want to have conference call with the four of you guys.'"

"'Your task is to go in there and find out how bad the situation is and what needs to be done.' About 10:00 I get a call from Lou Cannon, the *Washington Post* reporter who covered Reagan when he was governor. I knew Lou. And Lou says, 'Al, I'm calling not as a friend, but a reporter. We're – the Post is going to carry a front page story tomorrow that Burford has fired you. I want a confirmation. I said, 'Lou. Burford can't fire me. I've got a Presidential appointment,' and he said, 'well, I understand you had a very confrontational meeting with her today.' Now, Lou knew all of the background – and I said, 'Lou, she and I had a meeting and we need to discuss further what my role is going to be and – [being a] good old bureaucrat, you just cover yourself in this kind of way – and I said, 'what are your sources?' And he said 'Jim Baker.' He said if you deny it, we won't run the story. It ran three days later, but it was not on the front page."

After accepting the EPA position, Zuck recalls that he and the other appointees "were asked to do a review and meet with [Craig] Fuller at the White House in a very secretive meeting. None of us could be seen together and all this kind of thing. And they started off with me. 'Okay. What are your findings? What are your conclusions?' I said, 'hey, she's got to go and most of the political appointees have got to go. Well, that was concurred by the three other guys.' Two days later she resigned. That was my EPA episode."

In 1980, President Reagan appointed Raymond Donovan as Secretary of Labor. "When Reagan got elected, I was the Assistant Secretary for Administration and Management in the Carter Administration. He nominated a guy named Ray Donovan to be Secretary of Labor. Donovan was the head of the Schiavone Construction Company in New Jersey and had all kinds of trouble getting confirmed. So I was the Acting Secretary for a couple of months. When Donovan finally got confirmed – and he subsequently resigned a couple years after because there was a special prosecutor and all kinds of stuff, ties with the Mafia, et cetera. Donovan said to me, 'Hey, Al, I don't understand any of this. I'm told that Reagan is going to reappoint you as Assistant Secretary for Administration and Management. I don't understand how that's possible. You're a liberal Democrat. You worked for Hubert Humphrey, now this administration's 180 degrees different from that.'"

"Because I came up the career ladder, when I went into a political position, there is a provision that you can't be removed for a period of 120 days, to give some exposure and experience. He said, 'there's nothing I can do about you for 120 days, but let's go and see how this is going work.' The other thing he said is, 'the Congress, the Republicans in Congress are saying you are the one guy that needs to be retained here. Now that's because, I'm sure they were saying, 'hey, you need somebody who knows, I had a very strong hand in running that department. Within five days I was into a knock down drag out with Donovan because he wanted to award a sole source contract to the guy who ran the media effort of the Reagan campaign to do a study of the

Department of Labor's information office, public affairs activities, publications, et cetera. I said, 'No. That's big trouble. You just had problems getting confirmed. If you award the contract it's got to be announced in the Congress Business Daily. It's going to become public information and you're going to be back in the soup."

"Well, we hassled over that for about ten days, and his Chief of Staff, who was just a young jerk who had been in the advanced staff of the Reagan campaign, whose former job was a bartender, said to me, 'hey, don't you understand that there was a mandate given to have this contract signed? I mean Reagan got this mandate and this is a part of the mandate.' And he got so angry he said, 'All right. Put your damn reasons in writing.' And then I knew I had got them, because all of this was going to become public information."

"Well in the end, the contract never got done. But Donovan became a great fan of mine. When I left – I mean, I only stayed around with him two years [because] I was off to the EPA. He said at my retirement that of all of his inner staff, I was the only one who really protected his ass.'

That Zuck spent most of his career at the Department of Labor was purely by chance. "Actually my desire was to go to the budget bureau, but they weren't doing any hiring, and they said, 'hey, we've got a great spot, the first time the Assistant Secretary for Management in the Department of Labor was going to take an intern. We've been beating on her to do this. It's going to be a great spot because you'll be right in his office. They said, go there for a year. Maybe next year we can have an opening, which they did."

"But by then I didn't want to leave. First, one really had a broad access. I mean, that was one of my criteria. Where did I have this broad perspective? And I really got involved in the beginning. This was the Eisenhower administration. The beginning of progress – the era of redevelopment actually. We were beginning to retrain coal miners who were losing their jobs because of automation in the mines. So I really got involved in the beginning of what later became Employment and Training and there were others, the Manpower Development Act during the Johnson administration was really expanding those areas very extensively."

"Then I got involved in the appropriation process and with Congress. I testified for almost 20 years before those committees, and that's where I began to get all my access to leaders of the Congress. I developed a reputation among both Republicans and Democrats on the committee, as being somebody they could rely on and was a straight shooter. "

In addition to "cleaning up" the EPA and opposing conduct he believed inappropriate, Zuck had a distinguished career in Washington. He has served as Assistant Secretary of Labor for Administration and Management; Acting Secretary of Labor during the transition in 1981; Executive Director of the Commission on Executive, Legislative and Judicial Salaries; Comptroller for the Department of Labor from 1975 to 1977; Director, Administration and Management, Employment and Training Administration, Department of Labor, from 1970 to 1975; Director, Office of Evaluation, Employment and Training Administration, from 1968 to 1970; and Director, Federal Programs, President's Council on

Youth Opportunity, from 1967 to 1968. He also served in other positions at the Department of Labor beginning in 1958.

# Richard Kneedler – The College Is What It Is Today Because of Sidney

Over the last 50 years, Richard ("Dick") Kneedler has filled every role at F&M – student, alumnus, faculty, administrator, parent, spouse, and President of the College. Therefore, he has perhaps the best perspective on Sid Wise and his influence. For example, Kneedler looks back at one incident, in the fall of 1962, between his freshman and sophomore years, that had Sid Wise's fingerprints on it – the forced resignation of College President Frederick de Wolfe Bowman, Jr., and the decision by the Board of Trustees to unilaterally appoint Anthony R. Appel as the next president.

"At the time, the board was chaired by William Schnader, a Philadelphia lawyer. He was an old school controlling kind of guy, very loyal to the college, very generous," says Kneedler. Following Appel's appointment, which was engineered by Schnader, the new President appeared before the faculty to reassure them that he acknowledged their importance and need for professional independence. Following this statement, the faculty approved a motion of support by a voice vote.[4] Thereafter, the faculty approved a motion requesting that the Board of Trustees establish a joint trustee-faculty committee to select a new president. Following additional debate, and "[at] Sidney Wise's motion, a secret ballot was held on the previous motion of support for the new president. This time the vote was quite different: 23 for, 11 against, and 35 abstaining.

---

[4] *Liberalizing the Mind,* Sally F. Griffith, pp. 288-290.

The numbers reveal[ed] not only a lack of support for Appel but strong divisions with the faculty itself."

"Receiving such a ringing lack of endorsement, and hearing warnings from departmental chairmen that the college faced mass resignations by its best faculty if he remained, Appel resigned a week after his election." The subsequent president, Keith Spalding, would lead the College until 1982, and would count Sid Wise among his closest confidantes. Spalding was succeeded by James Powell, who led the College during a tumultuous period in which the College derecognized fraternities. Powell abruptly resigned in 1988, and was replaced by Dick Kneedler, who Powell believed "would be better able to deal with the aftermath of derecongition." Kneedler served as President of F&M until 2002.

Kneedler recalls the period in which Bolman was forced to retire – two years during which the College had four presidents, including interim leaders – as "the ultimate chaos." He notes that "in basically five or six days, the civil war was fought. The faculty faced down the board, the board backed off and the college became a modern college, and it would not have been if the board had continued to meddle in things that were well agreed by mainstream colleges and universities on how you do them. That board didn't get it. As a result, F&M would not have evolved in the way it did. It would not be the college it is now. It would be a very shaky place and not strong at all." Kneedler notes that "Sidney, I'm absolutely certain, had a central role of making sure that happened."

Kneedler also recalls when Professor Wise and other members of the faculty were held hostage by students unhappy with how the College handled the grading of exams in a course, the "Black Experience in America," claiming that they should themselves. "That was a much more unfortunate moment for him. It changed him and it changed him in ways that made him a less happy person. He was sad. He was disillusioned about things – it was a really bad time. He was used to an atmosphere of trust and collegiality. It was a kind of spit in your eye mindset that was going on and he became one of the missiles that was flying back and forth. It was aimed at him and it was really unfortunate. He never thought it should have happened."

"I think probably in some ways Sidney suffered a more profound disillusion out of it than most others did. It's very sad. It didn't ruin him as a teacher or a colleague or anything, but I think it fairly thereafter kind of colored the way he entered into collegial governance issues. There was a drawing of certain lines in the faculty. Not by Sidney by any means. It probably never entirely went away for some people. That was sad because it ripped the community. While the confrontation over the Bowman, Appel, and Schnader business created a cohesiveness in the faculty, I think the opposite happened with the Black Experience."

As a student, however, Kneedler did not take any government courses. Rather, he first got to know Sid Wise when he was a faculty member. Most of the time Kneedler spent with Wise was after he was a student and before he was President when he was a Professor of French and Assistant to then-Dean Vanderzell. In fact, he often ate lunch with Sidney and Dick Schier and others at their "famous" table in the Buchanan Room (the faculty dining room) in the College Center.

Kneedler remembers Wise's perspective on teaching government. "For Sidney it was not just the study of government, it was more of an art than a science, but it was really four square in the center of the liberal arts, which he saw as the best way to develop the power of the mind. His focus on internships was not a contradiction to that. It's rather the ultimate demonstration of the power of the liberal arts that people who have the general training of the mind and not a resolutely practical training, can go forth and do what the graduates of Sidney Wise's Government Department have done.

"When we revised the college's program in the 90s to move up the opportunity – individual opportunities is what we were calling them then – we had about 20 percent of our students doing some sort of honors or study abroad or similar program," Kneedler recalls. "We changed the faculty workload and came out with an agreement with the faculty that there would be a change in the way they would encourage individual opportunities through internships and tutorials and all those sorts of things. We moved that line from 20 percent of the student body to 75 percent of the student body. We were really emulating Sidney Wise. That's what we were doing. And Sidney did it – the government department did it with small numbers of faculty and large numbers of students. We never emulated that degree of efficiency college wide, but it was, particularly when you think about Sidney's career in its totality, it is a tremendous illustration of the liberal arts."

Kneedler adds that he does not know "who else would combine [Wise's] level of understanding of individuals, and his individual students, with his level of understanding of the overall environment which they faced, which is broad, national, and complex as can be. He was a smart person, and not a pretentious bone in his body. No pomposity at all. Just amazing, and amazing combination."

# Stanley Michalak – "You Work Behind the Scenes"

Stanley Michalak retired as The Honorable and Mrs. John C. Kunkel Professor of Government in June 2004 after having taught for 38 years at Franklin and Marshall College. Professor Michalak was also one of the most engaging lecturers at F&M, and many students have described him as the best lecturer they have ever heard at any school. He received his bachelor's degree magna cum laude from Albright College in 1960, and his Ph.D. from Princeton University in 1967. A recipient of the Christian R. and Mary Lindback Award for Distinguished Teaching, Professor Michalak focused his teaching and academic activities on international politics, international organization, American foreign policy, political ideologies, and urban issues, including crime and disorder.

When Sid Wise retired, Professor Michalak continued the tradition Sid Wise began of encouraging students to become involved in public service, regardless of their politics. While it is safe to say that Professors Michalak and Wise differed dramatically from each other in style, Professor Michalak learned much from his mentor/elder colleague and used that expertise to help numerous F&M students.

Professor Michalak first met Sid Wise in 1958, while still in college. At the time, the Rockefeller Foundation funded a group called The Citizenship Clearing House, whose goal, according to Michalak, was "to take the cream of the crop and get ten percent of the population to be really politically savvy and literate throughout the country." Professor Wise was asked to organize the central Pennsylvania region, and Stan Michalak arrived as one student in the group. "Then in 1959 they started the "First National Interns." We were the first Congressional interns in Washington and Sidney was in charge of Pennsylvania. There were six of us. I was in my Congressman's office and Sidney would come visit to see how we were doing."

While an intern, Michalak learned how to run a Congressional office. After graduation from Albright, he headed to Princeton and "absolutely hated it after one semester." Meanwhile, the Congressman for whom Michalak worked was re-elected, and he became the Congressman's assistant, overseeing the office's interns and developing a relationship with Professor Wise. "I went back to Princeton. I [then] went to Ohio State and he kept in touch. He said, 'Why don't you come and look at F&M because the College was beginning to expand in the '60s. So I came back. He showed me around the campus. I met Eileen Wise and I'm wowed because 'these guys are really good.' And I felt so completely at home here. The next year they asked if I wanted to come for an interview, and it went really well and I took the job. That's how I started in 1966."

After joining the faculty at F&M, Michalak and Wise worked closely together. Michalak noted that, as a colleague, Wise and the other government professors "let you do what you wanted to do. They gave you the presumption that you knew what you were going to do, and you did it."

After Wise retired, Michalak continued to help place students in internships and in jobs. "What you do is you watch, you get your seniors and you figure where you can place them. You determine who needs what and who's out there that can help them. The goal was getting them placed where they belong."

Michalak also recalls how Professor Wise, along with other Government professors, would work to accomplish political goals. For example, the Hamilton Club, a private club in Lancaster, "wouldn't let Blacks in. We told President Spalding, 'You have no choice, you have to get out. Now the question is whether you're going to get out now and resign and say the club's restrictions do not reflect the college's values. Or are you going to wait until the kids run around with signs decrying racism? Then you're going to have to back down and you will look like you did it out of pressure and you really were a racist." Within a matter of days, Spalding resigned. But then they still didn't take Jews. So the first open heart surgeon Lancaster General Hospital wanted to hire –Lawrence Bonchek from Milwaukee, who later served on F&M's Board of Trustees – wanted to join the Hamilton Club. So now all the WASPS had to decide whether they wanted an open-heart surgeon or no Jews in the Hamilton Club. Wow. Welcome."

Michalak recalls Wise's advice that "You work behind the scenes, you figure out who's there. You don't run around screaming and yelling." He recalls one situation in which students held Professor Wise and other professors hostage. They "couldn't leave until he agreed with them. Four or five professors were locked in Goethean Hall, and they were in there I guess for four or five hours taking votes. I don't know how the hell they got out. I guess the Dean offered the students amnesty. The profs then went to a faculty meeting. Wise went through the events and says, 'I think this is the saddest day in the history of the college.' Up pops some prof in the history department, who says 'This is one of the happiest days in the history of the college. Change is coming here. Revolution is coming here. We were off to the races.'"

"But, there was this terrible joke that they told after the Revolution remarks. Sidney always said you work within the system. So people in the history department would say, 'Here in Nazi Germany. Wise and Schier and some other guy are standing at the Firing Line Wall and the Nazis are ready to shoot them. Then the guy, the other guy, the third guy spits on the firing squad and yells epitaphs. And Wise says, 'don't rock the boat, play within the system.' When Sidney heard that, he said if *he* [the history professor] were in Nazi Germany, he'd be licking their ass on the way to the gas chamber thinking that they were friends,' because this guy was very, very pro-soviet you know. But Sidney was quick. When I told him that joke, he was that quick. His mind was razor sharp. He was really fast."

Professor Michalak notes that Professor Wise "taught [students] how to think, not what to think. An example of that is the Harrisburg Urban Semester. One student went there and wrote a paper on a bill to require fluoridation in urban water systems. She started out explaining fluoridation, what it is, the case for it, the case against, concluded with a chapter on why the state should fluoridate. Sidney says to her, 'did the bill pass?' She said 'no.' He said, 'Your job as a political scientist is not to tell me what we should do, but why such a wonderful idea – what you think is a wonderful idea here – could not get a majority of the votes in a State Legislature. I'll never forget that, because that says so well, and is such a good example of how you teach kids how to think, not what to think."

Noting the demise of civility in politics, Michalak says that "Sid believed in civility. That's gone. What we need in this country is a return to reason, discussion of problems and civility, which used to be conservative values. Politicians have lost their way. I can't believe it, but the civility is gone. [In the old days,] you problem solved. We can't even discuss our problems."

When Wise passed away, Michalak notes that the school lost "a fixture, a permanency, somebody who you could always go to. You know, when you're young and you always think the guys older than you know everything and you can always count on them. Of course, then you become the oldest, they're thinking that of you, and you say 'holy shit. What do I know?' But he was always there. If you had a problem, he always had good ideas."

"I guess I was really flattered when he had to make those tough medical decisions [about his health] at the end of his life. He would come in and go through the options with me, and say, 'what do you think about this, what do you think about this, what do you think about this?' I guess that really touched me, that he would have such confidence in me, to do that. What we lost when he died was a guy who read everything and forgot nothing. Charles Fox once said of Edmond Burke, 'I learned more from talking to Edmond Burke than I did from all the books I've read' and that's how I felt about Wise and Schier. They were so fast and so good and so quick in assessing a situation. The two of them together were just terrific."

Another change in the College that Professor Michalak credits to Professor Wise was the decision to accept female students. "The reason we went to co-education was that all the Ivy League schools had Jewish quotas up to the mid-60s. I have a friend, an oncologist. He had a 775 on the math in the SAT's. He went to Bronx Science and had a 750 on the English SAT and couldn't get into an Ivy League School. So what we at F&M were all these very, very bright Jewish kids who came in here and did premed. But then the quotas went away, and so did many of the bright kids. Now we had 400 boys, 200 of which were dummies. So Sidney's on the co-education committee, which created a new set of "women's majors," art, music, language. Then the women came and they were no different than the men. They wanted to be pre law, business, and science and go on to graduate and professional school. They want to do all that stuff. The women are just terrific. In essence, you got rid of 200 dummy boys and you got 200 bright women. That really picked the place up."

Many people describe Sid Wise's charisma. According to Michalak, "The word you want is not charisma. He had this quiet way. He never yelled, he never screamed, he never raised his voice. Sidney was really good on the quiet, because he was including you, talking to you and he made sense when he talked. You just felt welcome."

# Harvey Klehr – "A Great Teacher Really Requires A Special Kind Of Gift"

Considered one of the preeminent authorities on American Communism, Harvey Klehr never imagined as a high school student that he would attain such academic heights. In fact, while growing up in New Jersey, he wondered about how he would pay for college, not where his career would lead him. Now the Andrew W. Mellon Professor of Politics & History at Emory University, Klehr is the author of 14 books focusing on Communism, the American Left and the Cold War, countless articles, and the recipient of many awards, including the Thomas Jefferson, Scholar-Teacher of the Year, and the Emory Williams Distinguished Teaching Awards from Emory.

But in the early 1960s, such academic achievements were not even in his dreams. In fact, when Harvey Klehr decided to attend F&M, he selected the school because he "couldn't get a scholarship anywhere else." The son of immigrants, he was "first generation college, the oldest of three." While his parents "knew their kids were going to college, they had no concept of American higher education. It was foreign to them." The process was equally foreign to Klehr, who wanted to attend an Ivy League school, but "distinctly remember[s] that [in 1962] the guidance counselors wouldn't let me apply to most of them because there were still quotas at that time. For example, they would not let [him] apply to Princeton because there was another Jewish kid in the class that was applying to Princeton who was ranked one above [him]."

As a result, when Klehr graduated high school in 1963, he selected Franklin and Marshall. The choice was neither easy nor obvious. Klehr applied to numerous schools, ranging from Rutgers to other smaller schools and was accepted at all of them. His first choice was Tufts, but because the school did not offer him a scholarship, his choices were limited to Rutgers and F&M, both of which offered him a scholarship. Because he "really didn't want to go to Rutgers," Klehr went to F&M, although he "didn't know very much about it." In essence, his arrival "at F&M was totally by chance."

When Harvey Klehr arrived on campus, he wasn't sure what he would do with his life. "When I got there, I thought I wanted to be a lawyer because, you know, the Jewish parents and you're a doctor or a lawyer or you're a bum and that's, those were the alternatives," he recalls. "So I thought I was probably pre-med. But I was interested in politics."

During his first semester at F&M, Klehr took Gov 11, the introductory course in the Government Department, with Professor Vanderzell. Klehr recalls that the "class met at eight in the morning and it was the top floor of Old Main. [Professor] Vanderzell was the most intimidating guy. He scared me to death. Always dressed very nicely and he would have a cigarette dangling from his lip and smoke just billowing around his face. I remember [on] the first day he said, this class starts at 8:00 a.m. I'm here at 8:00 a.m. I expect you to be here at 8:00 a.m. and the door's closed."

"I'll never forget that first week or something. He starts at 8:00 and he closes the door. He starts lecturing and we hear somebody coming up the stairs and you could just hear them very slowly and Vanderzell stops talking and you see the doorknob slowly turn. Then Vanderzell suddenly yanks the door open and he says, oh Mr. Whatever. He always called people Mr. 'So nice to see you. We're so delighted you can join us. Would you like to come in? Come on in. How about that seat? Does that suit you?' You know, I mean the guy just wanted to shrivel up. That was the last person that was ever late for that class."

Klehr "loved the course and did well in it." He eventually took a course with Sid Wise. "It was a political theory course. By that time I knew who I was because it was a small department, Schier, Wise and Vanderzell, and they obviously talked to each other. I had done very well and so I think they sort of marked me as somebody that they were going to focus on."

Klehr recalls that Sid Wise "took a personal interest in people, [asking] 'What do I want to do?' I wanted to be a lawyer. 'Why do you want to be a lawyer?' Well I didn't know why I wanted to be a lawyer. He just slowly talked and he said, 'Have you ever thought about being a professor?' 'No,' was my answer," says Klehr. "He pulled me [aside] to discuss if I had ever thought about being a professor. He always was available if I had a question, and the stuff I was doing was really so far from his kind of interest. It was just the encouragement, the – 'We know you can do this. We know that you got the ability to do this.'"

"Being a professor was foreign to me. I never heard of people doing that and he talked about the kind of life it was and how enjoyable it was. I'm just this naïve, young kid, who has no idea what he wants to do in life. I thought, boy, that's kind of a neat life and secondly, you mean they pay you for reading books?

Certainly, by the end of my sophomore year I knew I wanted to be a college professor. It was not just Sid. I mean it was Vanderzell too and Schier. Although they certainly were willing to talk to you, Sid was just so avuncular. He took just such a personal interest in you. Come on, come in and talk, and he's the sweetest man."

"He sensed what people were good at or what they would be good at, and part of that came from the fact that he talked. He spent so much time talking to students and he really got a sense of who you were and what made you tick. He pushed me to do other kinds of things. Wise called me in and he said, 'Pittenger is looking for a research assistant and I'd think you'd be good at that. Is it something that you'd be interesting in doing?' 'Sure.' So Pitt took me up to Harrisburg when the Electoral College met in January. I did research for him, stuff he was working on in the legislature and he wound up directing my honor's thesis, "Multi-member Districts in Pennsylvania." At that time, Pennsylvania had multi-member legislative districts and the argument was that multi-member districts were created as a form of gerrymandering."

"It was a wonderful experience and I think for Sid it was sort of further confirmation of the fact that I belonged in the academy. He sat me down my senior year and said, 'Okay, you're interested in American politics, so let's talk about where you should go and who would be good to study with,' and he steered me. 'These are graduate schools that will be good for you' and I ended up at UNC."

"When I got my first job at Emory, I let him know. He was obviously very pleased. The first article I wrote appeared in the *Journal of Politics*. As soon as I got a reprint, I sent one to Sid and got back this letter that was glowing with such fatherly pride. It just made you feel really, really good, that you had vindicated his faith in you."

"When I became a college teacher, my model of what the college teacher was not the people that taught me in graduate school. It was Wise, Schier, and Vanderzell. I knew I could not be quite like that. I just don't have the kind of ease with people that Sid did. Somebody who really works at it can become a good solid teacher. But a great teacher really requires a special kind of gift and you can't train people to have that gift. Sid had that. I don't think that I necessarily have it but it's the kind of ideal that when I think about what kind of teacher I want to be or I ought to be or when I'm falling short, it becomes clear to me why. In my years in the department and my years as a department chairman, one of the things that always motivated me was that ideal, we want people to have concern for students. It's extraordinarily rare that anybody can have the kind of concern like Sid did. Sid focused on his students and their careers. He was just a rare human being and it's a rare combination of the right person, in the right place, with the right temperament and the right gift."

After graduating, Klehr remained in touch with Professor Wise. "There was a certain kind of loyalty that came from having gone to F&M. He was not shy about calling upon that loyalty. He would periodically call me up and say, 'We got a student who just discovered late in the game they're interested in graduate school. Can you help?' For a while at Emory, we had a pipeline of F&M students."

"I was just extraordinarily grateful and remain extraordinarily grateful. I think that without Sid, my life would have been totally different. That has very little to do with what he taught me in the classroom. I would not have gone down the career path that I went down. I don't think there's any doubt in my mind about that."

"I would send Sid copies of my books and he would talk about how proud he was that I was advancing in the profession and going some places in the profession that he never went. When they invited me back to campus to give a lecture, I was so extraordinarily proud that they would think that I was somebody that both they and students could learn from, and it was just one of the proudest moments in my life. Sid just had this unbelievable gift to an incredible number of the students he taught. They may not ever remember any of the content, but they remembered Sid and the impact that he had on their lives. Sometimes as direct in my case, other times indirect simply because there was just such a fundamental connection."

"Here was a guy, who was at a small liberal arts college, didn't publish. Everybody knew him. All the biggies in the profession knew Sid. That's awfully rare because those people know, even somebody's been around for a while, if they haven't published, they're nobody."

# Mark Weinheimer – "Politics Is The Art Of The Possible"

A 1968 graduate of F&M, Mark Weinheimer is a consultant and the founder of Weinheimer & Associates in Washington, D.C. focusing on community development and management. A Philadelphia native, Weinheimer was encouraged to go to F&M because of his involvement in politics while in high school.

During his four years at F&M, Weinheimer "became less interested in politics per se and more interested in policy and government, the governing as opposed to the politics end of it. Sid Wise arranged an internship – you know his famous internship program – and [he] ended up for a summer in Washington." Weinheimer interned for the Americans for Democratic Action during his sophomore and junior years, and was the first sophomore who served as an intern in Washington at Sid Wise's behest.

During the summer of 1967, Sid Wise helped Weinheimer "make a connection with the city of Lancaster. [He] did a summer internship for the city working for the mayor doing special projects and working for the redevelopment agency. Then after graduation [he] went back there because [he] was more interested in actually governing at that point. The political stuff was less interesting.

Weinheimer "stayed in the public sector for about ten years, working for two cities and state government." Then he worked for the Department of Housing and Urban Development at the end of the Carter administration before leaving government.

Although he is no longer in government, his firm focuses on community development and he remains "very involved with government programs, advising" governments, not being involved in the politics aspects.

In this role, Weinheimer was closely involved in the creation of the National Community Development Initiative (NCDI), which began in 1991 as a $250-million 10-year-long effort underwritten by 18 national funders, including foundations, lenders, insurance companies and HUD, to enhance the work of community development corporations (CDCs). NCDI has transformed itself into "Living Cities," a national consortium of private and public funders that helps to improve the lives of low-income people and the cities where they live.

Through 1997, the NCDI has pooled over $150 million from corporate, philanthropic, and government sources in an effort to increase the capital available to CDCs – often the most productive developers of affordable housing for a city's low-income residents. Two intermediary organizations, the Local Initiatives Support Corporation and the Enterprise Foundation, worked with local partnerships in the 23 cities studied to invest NCDI funds in CDCs. In its more than 20 year existence, NCDI has invested approximately $1 billion, which it leveraged into over $16 billion, in America's cities.

Weinheimer first met Sid Wise when he was assigned to him as his freshman academic advisor; he also was Weinheimer's Government 101 professor. The two "hit it off immediately." Weinheimer credits Sid with keeping him at F&M because "Growing up in Philadelphia, making the transition to Lancaster was not easy. I told him I wanted to transfer to either a Philly school or a Washington school. Wise encouraged me to stick it out and apply for a scholarship. All of a sudden in the mail appeared this scholarship to stay at F&M. As a result, I figured I'd stay." At F&M, Weinheimer was a government major, and President of the Gov Club. He was also student manager of the film series for about a year, and he would see Sid daily. In fact, because of his government service, Weinheimer remained in Lancaster for four years after graduation.

Weinheimer recalls that although he had practical political experience from his high school days, Sid Wise introduced him "to the literature of political science and government and made [him] more interested in the governing side. It [became] more of a discipline than just a strange hobby." Weinheimer recalls that Wise was also "very involved in the personal life, in the good way, of the students. Of course, one of the benefits of a small college, you got to meet the professors and they met you and you could relate to one another. But he took an interest in folks and understood what their goals were and could – through internships and otherwise – help get them connected. For example, my second internship with the city was not through his formal program, but through connections he had with the mayor."

Currently, Weinheimer works "with a lot of nonprofit organizations that are doing housing, economic development, helping them on development and evaluation, strategic planning ... [he helps] devise programs, develop programs, or run programs. [He also performs] program assessment work, has helped regional foundations put together public-private programs, and worked with the local government to put joint programs together, including multi-year funding of community activity, community organizing, and community development."

Weinheimer also learned about networking from Sid Wise, in particular "making sure you don't drop people, and maintain your networks." In addition, he recalls Wise's description of politics "as part of the art of the possible. We talked about being careful of things going too far. If you start a protest, where does it end? After you change the Hamilton Club, and if that's your goal, fine, great. Then it can't go beyond that to overthrow city government or whatever. You don't know where these things will go. It was the protesting within the normal bounds of the political system."

# Harold Dunbar – "He Always Had A Sense That He Knew Where To Direct People"

Harold Dunbar's record of public service symbolizes the type of career Sid Wise envisioned for many of his students. But like so many other F&M alumni, Wise's influence on this 1969 graduate goes further. When he arrived at F&M, Dunbar's primary goal was to prove to himself that he could be the good football player he wasn't in high school. At F&M, he was on the football team with Earl Devaney, broke school records as a running back, and became a self-acclaimed BMOC (Big Man on Campus). He was also a founder of the Afro-American Society. After graduating from F&M, Dunbar attended and graduated from the University of Virginia Law School, and then began a career in government service. He is currently Chief Deputy Attorney General of Pennsylvania, where he heads the Civil Rights Enforcement Section. When he arrived at F&M, such a career seemed a pipe dream.

"I'm the first person in my family to have the opportunity to graduate from college," Dunbar explains. In those days when you were thinking about attending colleges, you would go to a college night that they would have at some local high school where various admissions representatives would be there to interview you, to make suggestions, whatever the case may be."

"We accidentally bumped into an admissions person from Franklin and Marshall and I just had a brief conversation with him and he mentioned that Varo Duffins, who was an African American from the Harrisburg area, had been a freshman that year and he recommended that I come by and listen to his interview about, the discussion about the college."

"This was the time of social upheavals and the riots that were taking place. Schools were reaching out, some of them for the first time, in a very significant way to increase their African American students. So I listened to what he had to say. I was very much impressed by the reputation of the school."

"It just so happened that I was a football player in high school here, and I realized that I wasn't going to the NFL, so I wasn't trying to get into Notre Dame, and Franklin and Marshall just happened to be the kind of school that met what I thought were my goals. I visited the campus. In fact, I visited all the schools I applied to. I visited West Chester State, Howard University and Franklin and Marshall."

"As it turned out, West Chester offered me a full athletic scholarship, Howard offered me a half and half type deal, half athletic scholarship, half academic scholarship. Franklin and Marshall would not offer me any scholarship at all. It was the most expensive of the three schools and I decided to go there notwithstanding, because I was so much impressed with the school and the character of the school and the way it looked, the location of the school and so forth."

"So at the age of 17, in 1965, I headed off for Franklin and Marshall College. I can remember it like it was yesterday. We were going down to the orientation program. I think the college was in part interested in me because of my athletic ability also. They wanted that then. Obviously students had to meet certain academic standards but they wanted people who could actually make a contribution to the school in some unique way, and I was asked at my interview whether I would come out for the football team and I said that I would."

After Dunbar selected F&M, he came to campus. "One of the things that was true was that we were in one of the first classes where appreciable numbers of African Americans attended the College. There had been a number before – I've gotten to know about some of these people two or three at a time, but in our class they had about 20.

"I was a government major, why I don't know, but I just felt that government would be the most appropriate thing to me because I was interested in politics. Dr. Wise was a supporter of the athletic department, and the football program in particular, and he was one of these guys who recognized that we were only kids, and that we might really like football, but there could be a problem with football or whatever sport, interfering with the academic part of college."

"His approach to me was to remind me that I wasn't going to the NFL, and to remind me that my father was very serious about a number of warnings he had given me, to stay out of trouble and stay on course. He was very very helpful all the way."

Dunbar recalls Wise as "a very bright man intellectually, a very knowledgeable person politically. But I think he was most interested in how politics actually worked. What came out of it? What could come out of it? As opposed to the structure of politics. To give you an example of what I'm talking about, there was a precinct in Harrisburg, and in the Goldwater election it was the only black precinct in the nation that voted for

Barry Goldwater. Not only did this particular precinct go for Barry Goldwater, but it did by 104% of the vote. I know Dr. Wise and Dr. Schier were both interested in finding out how that happened. Did I have any insights how this happened to take place in Harrisburg?"

In addition, Dunbar recalls that Wise "said something about Adam Clayton Powell, who really disappointed him, because here was a black man capable enough to have a Congressional district created in the first place, and then rise to be the Ways and Means Chairman, and he basically blew it as a result of a fraud and the other things, including malfeasance. Sid always talked about how much good a guy like that did and could do in that position and how wasteful it really was for him to dissipate his power and end up losing his seat altogether."

Dunbar recalls Wise helping African-American and other minority students. "I don't know if he was color blind. I think he's one of these people who was progressive. He realized that there were some issues. He also realized that as a result of Jim Crow laws in the South and the African American history in this country, that there were some systemic issues, and that one way to deal with that would be to encourage people who he thought had the ability to go further, and to set their goals higher."

"I never felt that he was attracted to me so much because I was African American, however. He liked my personality and he thought I could be successful and I was also an athlete and I was one of the chosen ones, I guess," Dunbar recalls, noting that Wise suggested that he consider the CLEO (Council on Legal Education Opportunity) program." "I would never have known about CLEO. Because he got involved with internship programs, that he got people into, it was like he always had a sense that he knew where to direct people."

"There was an Upper Bound program that actually went the other way. They were identifying kids in high school that had – pretty much along racial lines, but that they thought had the ability to do well at college and F&M was the regional institution for the Upward Bound program. A number of kids at Harrisburg eventually were admitted into F&M as a result of that Upward Bound program. I wasn't one of them. I was before that time."

"Again, they were people that were very progressive. You know, it was during the time of the Civil Rights Movement. In context, this was the time when Dr. King was out there. Malcolm X was out there. The Student Non Violent Coordinating Committee was out there. So that was the context out of which these things took place. "

"The other thing I really remember was the takeover of the palace. They wanted to take over a palace. Somehow we – first of all, this was the first Black Student Union, it was African American Societies. When we started out, it was named African American Society. A number of the brothers, so to speak, convinced the College to offer a course and I think it was pretty much the Black Experience or the African American Experience. Something along those lines."

"And these guys thought it was great because grading was very tough at F&M in those days. They never try and flunk people out, but very, very few As were given in any course. So these guys were under a lot of pressure, and they wanted this course because they thought that it should be offered, and that they would do well in it. Well, I didn't take the course for whatever reason, but as it turned out the opposite [happened]. They discovered that the highest grades were going to non-African American students and these guys just went berserk. I mean, they couldn't believe that that could possibly happen."

"Now, in retrospect, I knew that it could happen. But these guys started losing it. Now, again, this was during the time of takeovers at various institutions, so, that was the thing to do. The idea initially was that they were going go up to the government department, where all the professors were and talk about this thing. But apparently, one thing led to another and the next thing I know, I'm over at the geo lab trying to fit this last science course that I had to get in order for me to graduate, and a guy comes in there and says, you know, Harold, your father's on the phone. He says to me, 'I hope you're not involved in that stuff.' And I said, what, what, what? What are you talking about? Then he said, you remember your deal with me. You're going to graduate from school and you're going to do it in four years. I said, yeah, and he said, well, it's been on the news that students are taking over offices, professors' offices on campus."

"I said, well, I don't know anything about that, dad, and I'm going to look into that, because that certainly was not supposed to happen based on this agreement that we had to support each other. So I got out there, and I'm telling you, in one way it was one of the most – the funniest thing you ever seen in your life. I mean, these guys wouldn't hurt a fly, and they were walking around out in front of the offices and I think there'd been at least one interview from a reporter from a paper. They had the professors locked in the offices and they weren't going to let them out until they got these grades straightened out. That was my experience."

"I was able to convince these guys to back off before some serious trouble went down, like the National Guard being called to campus. I was one of the key agents in diffusing the situation. [Sid] was one of the leaders in diffusing the immediate problem, and also getting [it] eventually resolved. It may not seem like such a big deal now, but then it was because it was a continuation of that kind of problem that eventually led to Kent State.

"So I think I was fairly intellectual, and most of the students and I realized it was a serious mistake and I was able to convince these guys to back off before some serious trouble went down. Like the National Guard being called to campus. It was obviously all over the news so the authorities had to do something because people had to know about it. I kind of was an agent; maybe everybody doesn't have that memory that I have, but I was one of the key agents in kind of diffusing the situation."

"Subsequently, after the duress was off, and people could deal rationally, there was some kind of accommodation with these guys. They didn't get the As and the Bs they wanted, but they passed the course and it counted as extra credit." Dunbar recalls that Dr. Wise was one of the professors he approached about the situation. "They were not going to let this thing go and get out of hand. We would not – there were enough of us who are not going to let this thing get out of hand so that law enforcement has to be involved."

"There were two big stories I had about [Sid]. Two big stories. The one was CLEO, the Council of Legal and Educational Opportunity. Their main objective was to increase the number of African American lawyers in the country. In order to do that, they set up programs on a regional basis. You would apply to the school, to the law school – I applied to the University of Virginia. Actually I hadn't applied to the University of Virginia. The regional program was at the University of Virginia. I was selected and I was chosen to be part of that. Then over the course of about a month and a half, you actually went to the school."

"There were preliminary courses that were given. Outstanding professors from all different law schools taught these courses. They basically tested you and filtered out those that they thought could be successful from those who would not be successful. As a result of qualifying, you got a substantial scholarship as well. Dr. Wise brought that program to my attention, and that's how I ended up at the University of Virginia Law School. That was how I ended up getting accepted at every law school I applied to, The University of Virginia, University of Texas, Vanderbilt University and Temple University, as a result of being involved in that program. I can't say any more about the significance of that experience."

"I have benefited immensely from my education at Franklin and Marshall; it was one of the smartest moves that I ever made. I've got to say the government department in particular had outstanding teachers. Dr.

106

Schier, Dr. Vanderzell, as well as Dr. Wise, were just outstanding people."

# William (Bill) R. Lloyd, Jr. – Don't Take It Personally

A 1969 F&M graduate, Bill Lloyd graduated from Harvard Law School in 1972, and served from 1981 to 1998 in the Pennsylvania House of Representatives. From approximately 2002 to 2013, he served as the Small Business Advocate for Pennsylvania, and is a now a private attorney. Sid Wise once told me that Bill Lloyd should one day be governor of Pennsylvania. However, he never achieved that position in 1998 when he lost the U.S. Senate election to incumbent Arlen Specter.

Lloyd's political transition and his relationship with Sid Wise are equally fascinating. "When he left F&M, [Lloyd] was still a liberal Republican, although [his] first presidential vote [was] for Hubert Humphrey. I still remember standing in one of the dining halls on election night in 1968, standing next to Sid and it [had] come down to Ohio. He said something about not liking to be counting on Ohio," a state whose influence remains in Presidential elections.

As it did for so many other students, F&M had a profound impact on Lloyd. "I'm not sure that I can connect the dots to any specific thing. But I was a small town boy, somewhat naïve and applying to go to college. I went to a college where all these people were from Philadelphia or New York or Boston. I went to college where there were a whole bunch of people whose religious persuasion was not mine and it was kind of my growing up. I was at a school where I was editor of the newspaper. Yet I could be involved in things because it was a small enough school."

Lloyd's relationship with Sid also increased after college. "He got in touch with me and he started having me come down to talk to one of his classes. I would go down to his classes, and he would interview me. He would ask questions to get me to talk about the things he wanted students to hear in the hope that that would then prompt questions from them. He also had a book on the legislative process, and that was in his book. Lloyd recalls that Sid Wise and Dick Schier "always described themselves as due process liberals. Process mattered to them. You can talk to people on the other side of the aisle who were helped by Sid Wise. I don't know if you can find people like that [today. That's why] I think that his reaction [to modern politics] would have been that we're going in the wrong direction."

"Today, everything is based on tearing down – you can't disagree with the other guy," he says. "You have to tear him down. You have to belittle. One of the first things I learned when I was in the legislature was not to take it personally, that there were people who were going to vote against me on some issue, and they had reasons. Tomorrow, the guy who was against me today might be my biggest ally, because tomorrow I might try and do something that helps his district."

As result of his relationship with Sid and F&M, Lloyd developed an "attitude toward government that politics is the art of compromise and it's the art of what's possible. Well here's where you are. Here's where I am. We overlap that much. We have got to at least be able to do what we overlap. And then maybe we can negotiate. We can push that out a little bit. You give a little, I give a little. At least be able to do something. But the attitude seems to be – and I don't blame this just on the Republicans – the attitude now seems to be if we can't get what we want, we don't want anything at all. I mean we don't have to agree on everything at all, but we have to [if] we want to build highways, patch the potholes. That takes money. So if you're willing to vote and I'm willing to vote, well we work together and try to get enough other guys who are willing to vote. I don't like the way things have happened and I suspect Sid would agree."

# Jon Plebani – "The Linkage Between The Life Of The Mind And Political Activism"

Director of Federal Government Relations for a Washington, D.C. law firm, Jon Plebani in many ways has had the type of career typical of many F&M graduates. Before joining the law firm, Plebani was executive vice president of a government affairs firm. In 1994, he served as the deputy special advisor to the President on Haiti, and was the principal day-to-day contact for the White House with Haitian President Jean Bertrand Aristide. From 1992 to 1994, he served as chief of staff for House majority Whip William H. Gray, III and was responsible for the operation of the Whip organization that comprised more than 50 senior members of the House. From 1985 to 1988, he was Congressman Gray's staff director.

Plebani's relationship with government began when, at age 14, he worked as a page. Eventually, he went to Franklin and Marshall, at the suggestion of John Pittenger. Although he never took a course with Professor Wise, he "spent virtually every afternoon of [his] junior and senior years in Dick [Schier]'s office." They also made other connections. "They pawned [him] off as a speech writer in the United States Senate campaign in '70." Then, in 1976, Gene Knopf, Chief of Staff for Pennsylvania Lieutenant Governor Ernie Kline, "who had been an intern in a program that Sid had supervised," hired Plebani. He eventually became Chief of Staff to Congressman Allen Ertel. Of note, "over the years [Plebani's offices] hired a lot of Franklin and Marshall people."

Like other students, Plebani recalls Wise's efforts to force President Spalding to give up his membership in the Lancaster-based Hamilton Club. "I was head of something called The Committee For Human Rights. It was right around the assassination of Martin Luther King and Bobby Kennedy. We were casting about for some way to involve the social action, and were involved in helping an impoverished area of Lancaster. At the time, the president of the college, Keith Spalding, was a member of the Hamilton Club, which had a long history of excluding both African Americans and Jews. So it seemed appropriate that if you're going to do anything, that was one of the things that might be a positive thing the Committee for Human Rights too. I think I was elected chairman so of course that's the first thing I went after with that. I remember, with Sid's encouragement – I had a column in the newspaper so I went after the president saying essentially it was inconsistent with his role."

"In talking to Sid about how to do this, [Sid suggested contacting] Bob Sarnoff, who was chairman of the board of trustees, and chairman of RCA, which owned NBC at the time. So I'm this kid from Franklin and Marshall, but I just called Sarnoff's office every day – not virtually but every day, every business day for a month and finally he took the call. I was all prepped with Sid's encouragement to tell him that I thought it was wrong that the president of the college belonged to a club that the chairman of the board of trustees couldn't belong to. I remember that Sid was also doing things behind the scenes. Finally one day Kenny Duberstein [the President's assistant] called me over there to tell me that Spalding was resigning."

Plebani also recalls the "aura" of being a government major. "They were politicians in their own right, faculty politicians, but they were pleasant guys. Dick would always tell me about Sid driving a laundry truck when he was an undergraduate as a way of making money. You felt a part of some tradition there; you certainly felt a part of being a government major, which I mean – maybe the kids who were pre-meds felt the same way about being pre-meds – but there was a certain aura, a certain luster to being a government major and being one of the people that was close to the big three, who were Vanderzell, Schier, and Wise."

"The sense was that [Wise and Schier] had been in public service, both had worked for Senator Clark. Dick had been Deputy Secretary of Education in Pennsylvania. Sid and he continued to be active in the Democratic Party in Pennsylvania. So you get this sense that first of all, that kind of doing something else, whether it's practicing law, being a college professor and all that, is completely compatible with involvement in government, public service and politics. That was the ethos of the department, that it wasn't just this sort of insular academic community but that what was fun and inspiring was this connection to a broader world out there, and that there actually was some linkage between the life of the mind and that political activism. So we were very much a part of that – I think it was always, everybody if they were really close to them assumed that you do both in some way."

113

# Stanley Brand – "I Was An English Major Until Sid Adopted Me"

One of Sid Wise's protégés was Stanley Brand, who graduated from F&M in 1970 and majored in English, not Government. Mr. Brand received his law degree from Georgetown University in 1974, after which he entered public service. From 1976 to 1983, Mr. Brand served as General Counsel to the US House of Representatives under Speaker Thomas P. "Tip" O'Neill, Jr. In that position, he was the House's chief legal officer and was responsible for representing the House, its members, officers and employees in connection with legal procedures and litigation arising from the conduct of their official activities.

Since founding a Washington, D.C.-based law firm in 1983, Stanley Brand has "specialized in cases at the intersection of politics, criminal law and communicating in the Washington echo chamber," according to former client George Stephanopoulos in his best-selling autobiography "All Too Human: A Political Education" (Little Brown and Company, 1999). In 1984, he founded the Brand Law Group. His firm's practice focuses on defending the rights of witnesses involved in government investigations. He has also represented numerous individuals and organizations investigated by and/or called upon to testify before Congress. Since 1992, he has also served as Vice-President of the National Association of Professional Baseball Leagues, the governing body of minor league baseball. In that capacity, he was responsible for representing minor league baseball during congressional consideration of baseball's antitrust exemption and is responsible for minor league baseball's government relations at the state and local level. He has testified, written and lectured extensively on antitrust, labor and contract law issues affecting baseball. In 2005, Mr. Brand represented Major League Baseball in connection with the congressional investigation into MLB's steroid policies.

He also supervises the Semester in Washington internship program at the Penn State Dickinson School of Law. But when he came to F&M, Mr. Brand never imagined that his career would take such a direction. "I was interested in government from high school. It was something I'd always been turned on by, it was politics," Brand recalls. My father was a labor guy from New York who was heavily involved in New York City politics at a very sub-rosa level, but that's how it worked in those days, and so I went and I took this course."

"And it was this guy, Sid Wise, and one of the books in the syllabus was his book about formation of government and his time in the Senate with Joe Clark, and blah, blah, blah, and I found him fascinating. So I decided, well, maybe I should be a government major. So I take Government 11. Then I take Government 12, which is comparative government."

Despite his love of government, Brand was unsure of what his major would be. "I was an English major until Sid adopted me," he recalls. "He emblazoned real politics into my mind. He [was] an intellectual, but he [was] also a real pol. He encouraged students to get involved in real politics, and roll up their sleeves and work in campaigns."

"Anyway, at the same time – so I take those two courses and I'm pretty much headed on the path to being a government major. My sophomore year I have to plug a hole in my schedule, and I can't get into anything that I want. I go to the registrar and she says well, there's this course, in English, Introduction to Poetry. There's this new guy coming named Sandy Pinsker. Everybody says he's great. She said that one thing I'll warn you about is, this is like for English majors what organic chemistry is for pre-meds. I went, oh boy. I always like English. I'll take it. Well I get in the course, and Pinsker's just the guy – he opened up a whole world to me."

Meanwhile, Sid served as a "sort of ad hoc advisor to a lot of people, [including] me. So I went to see Sid and I said I'm torn, I just love this English stuff, and without missing a beat, he said, 'Hey, you got to do what you really like. He said take the government courses, you could be a biology major and go to law school if that's what you ultimately decide you want to do. So that's what I did."

"So I was an English major, but I maintained the relationship with him. He was sort of the advisor without portfolio. He was the default guy that I would go to if I had some ideas" Brand explains. In addition, he was influenced by the events occurring while he was in college. "Now remember, I graduated in 1970, which was the, probably the most tumultuous year in American college experience in 60 years. The war in Vietnam was raging. Kent State occurred literally a month before our graduation. The campus, relatively speaking for Lancaster, was in an uproar. Not as much as some of the other schools."

And Sid was kind of in there politically to vent to and also, I wouldn't say tamp down. That's too negative, but to maintain some semblance of academic regularity in a very difficult environment. There he was; he was like the presence there. We talked a good deal about it. I wasn't very active in that time as sort of a protestor. I was worried about the lacrosse season and the graduating and everything else but – so then I graduated and actually took time off. I didn't apply to law school. Got a job."

"And then I came down [to Washington] and I pounded the pavement for about three months and I got a job on Capitol Hill with then Congressman, about to be Majority Whip, Tip O'Neill, through a woman I had met and interviewed with. So I get this job low level, entry job, in O'Neill's office and of course I maintained the contact with Sid, and I'd go up to visit with him and take my wife and, so it was a lifelong relationship."

"Then I went to law school at night while I was working for O'Neill. I left when I graduated. I went to the SEC for two years. I was actually on a completely different path. Sort of corporate securities work. But Tip O'Neill called and said, 'Karl Albert's retired. I'm going to be speaker. I'd like you to come back, which I did.'"

"I kept the relationship up with Sid and I'd go back to campus. Duberstein and I went back a couple of times and did dog and pony shows. Duberstein, of course, became Chief of Staff to Reagan. I'd go back, almost, I'm sure once a year to see him or do a talk with the students. That was it."

But Sid Wise's influence extended further. He had numerous students and former students working in Washington. "People say that Sid Wise created this sort of Washington connection old-boy, old-girl network,"

117

Brand explains. "He did so much more. He was so much more of a force on campus in a lot of different ways. This is a guy who brought Franklin Schaffner back to campus. The stuff he did for a small college like that was phenomenal. Across the lines. It wasn't just government, it was cultural, it was social."

"If you looked at the types of people that he brought in, not just the films, but the people to speak, and the people to present issues and ideas about the films, it was just a whole separate curriculum that he invented in his spare time. It had nothing to do with government." Moreover, students stayed in touch and cultivated the connection with Sid and Government Department. "There's a whole second and third generation of people who also had Sid Wise connections," Brand recalls. "He was the default guy that I would go to if I had some ideas. It became, as Ken likes to say, a two way street where [Sid] would say, 'Well I'm the student now and you're the professor.' It was a lot of that for sure."

Like Duberstein, Brand continues to hire interns and provide guidance to F&M students. "I see hundreds of them during the year asking for advice; they want to go into baseball, they want to go into politics, they want to go into law. [I tell them], 'Find your passion and follow it, and everything else will work out.'"

"People are always trying to plot their careers, and I guess age has given me a certain perspective, where I say, don't be so worried about plotting every little move. Go where you feel passion. Go where you really want to go, and the rest will take care of itself. I think that's what [Sid] was saying, and that's certainly something I live by and it has served me well. I think he knew in some sense that people who followed their passion would be successful. Which, when you're the age we were in college, is not easy to know; there's a lot of choices. It's very competitive. It's probably worse today."

"People like Sid Wise translated that [college] experience into something larger. The part that I remember of his is his Renaissance man approach. He wasn't overly focused on any one thing. He was interested in a lot of things. He worked for a Democratic Senator [and] came from a fairly traditional Democratic perspective. But that wasn't part of what he did in this school. He fostered a non-partisan approach, and all of us, including in our relationships with each other – because we're obviously of different stripes – reflect that."

"I think he believed in the clarifying power of debate and discourse. That's how he thought things would resolve themselves. He certainly came by it naturally. It was just an old style view that the opposition wasn't the enemy. Coalitions had to be made. Majorities were created out of consensus."

"What I learned from people like Sid and more so from Tip O'Neill – for Tip O'Neill, spending a lot of time with someone was never a waste of time. Because there was some connection, some glimmer of something important that could come from that later on. I really watched him – an endless procession of people go into his office with nothing particularly important on their minds, and he'd listen and he'd talk and give them their due, and then somewhere down the road, somehow, that would work out in a way that redounded to his benefit. He just liked sitting around listening to people's stories and connecting up with them. I took a page out of that book. Whatever success I've had professionally has been largely a result of that. That's the way you connect to people and the way you succeed in life is the more people you connect to, the more people you can draw on later on. I saw that certainly with Sid, and with O'Neill. Maybe it's not happenstance that those are the people I've been drawn to, but very much the same."

"What Sid also did through indirection is he fostered a Washington network among us of all stripes. That is as deep, as inside, as any school in the country. There's no school in the country of like size that has the type of esprit de corps among its alumni. Gentlemen disagree agreeably. We all have high esteem for each other. The fact that we're of totally different stripes doesn't get in the way of that. That's the Sid Wise coda. You have to make compromises. You have to get something done that works a change or effects a change."

"That's how you imbue a culture into an institution, whether it's a school or a corporation or a political entity, and he is part of that. He is part of the culture created at F&M that is now being expanded and marketed on a much grander scale in a way that's very unique."

# Earl Devaney – "I'm Not the Most Famous of All His Kids"

His name is not well-known. In fact, he was always low key, so low key that his picture does not even appear in his College Yearbook. You can find his photo as a member of the football team, however, but that does not tell you anything about the man. While he may not be a household name, Earl Devaney is someone who helped change the entire culture of Washington, and was viewed during his career as a man of integrity who cared not a whit about politics.

So, who is Earl Devaney? He graduated from F&M in 1970, and was a government major. From there, he joined the Secret Service and was assigned to Vice President Gerald Ford's detail. He was present when President Richard Nixon resigned and boarded the helicopter at the White House. Devaney even took a bullet for President Ford when a gunman mistook the former lineman for the President.

Devaney retired from the Secret Service in 1991 after serving as the head of the agency's fraud division. He then joined the Environmental Protection Agency as Chief of Criminal Enforcement and was in charge of all of the agency's criminal investigations. In 1998, President Clinton awarded him the Meritorious Presidential Rank Award for his public service. He then became Inspector General at the Interior Department, where he led the investigation into Deputy Secretary J. Steven Griles and uncovered the illegal conduct of lobbyist Jack Abramoff. The investigation eventually led to Abramoff's imprisonment, the resignation of Griles for lying under oath about his own role in the scandal, and to 21 other persons either pleading guilty or being found guilty, including White House officials, one Congressman, nine other lobbyists and Congressional aides.

In September 2007, while still at the Interior Department, Devaney released a report that highlighted unlawful practices at the agency's Minerals Management Service (MMS), which oversaw natural resources on the continental shelf, and collected billions of dollars annually in royalties from oil and gas companies. Devaney's report recommended disciplinary action for employees at MMS who received gifts from oil companies; it also accused one management official of having sex with his subordinates, as well as purchasing cocaine while on the job. The report concluded that two other female employees had relationships with customers of the MMS, but did not recuse themselves from their lovers' companies' contracts.

Devaney also used to keep an alligator head in his office, yet another symbol of his success at fighting corruption. Inside the alligator head was a camera that was used to take pictures of an official taking bribes while on a fishing trip in the Louisiana bayou. Devaney explained to the *New York Times* that "When an assistant secretary comes in and asks about it, I tell that story and they get a little unnerved."

The final step in Devaney's career was as Chairman of the Recovery and Accountability Board, more commonly known as the Stimulus Program under President Barrack Obama. In that role, Devaney was tasked with preventing corruption, a goal viewed as impossible by many. But according to Michael

Grunwald, author of *The New Deal,* experts said 5 to 7 percent of it would be lost to fraud and so far it's been .0001 percent lost to fraud."[5]

Devaney credits his career path to Sid Wise. "I may represent a sort of a 'B' team kind of Sid Wise protégé; certainly not as famous as some of the ones, but nonetheless, in government for [over 40] years. I got some really good influence from Sid when I was in school, but as I was leaving school I went to him about career choices; and of course, Sid said government service was a worthy thing to aspire to," Devaney recalls.

"I had been a summer cop up at Cape Cod, and I kind of liked law enforcement," he explains. "The Secret Service gave me the opportunity to get into law enforcement, and it was a heavy connection to government and the presidency. I had an opportunity to go into the Secret Service because I applied, and I'd also applied to law school. So I went to Sid with this dilemma, and I was going to be passing up law school to go directly into government, and I wanted to know what he thought. Of course, he said all the right things: 'What do you want to do? It's not about making money. If you go to law school, you can always go into government, but here's an opportunity to go directly into government, you don't have to be a lawyer, and you can probably have a great career in government without being a lawyer.'"

Devaney pondered the advice and made his decision. "I went back to him about a week later and

---

[5] "What Did the Stimulus Do for States," *Governing,* December 2012, p. 11.

said, 'I've decided to go into the Secret Service.' For me, he was a sounding board during a pretty critical time in my life. I don't think my dad, for instance, who I went to for other things, could have provided advice that was as meaningful; as a matter of fact, my dad wasn't real happy I wasn't going to law school. But I never felt that I didn't make the right choice."

As a young agent, Devaney learned how accurate Wise was when he said that the Secret Service would provide an opportunity not available in law school. "So here I am a young Secret Service agent, and one of my first assignments is driving former Vice-President Hubert Humphrey, and I don't know where we were, maybe Los Angeles during the campaign, and driving along, and I'm listening to Humphrey and somebody, some state guy from California in the back seat, and their trading favors for a bill – they are going to, let's just say hypothetically, we're going to get a bill to build a road in California, and I'm going to do this for you; and I said to myself, quietly because you don't talk, just listen – 'Okay, now I get it, this is how things really happen in American government, it's in the back seat of this car, there's a chit-for-chit going across the table here – it's not corrupt, it's just the way the government works,'" Devaney recalls.

"And so later, I observed that that bill was passed, and I felt like I understood then how government really works. Nothing has dissuaded me from that notion since as to how government works. It's all trades and trade-offs, compromises. Essentially at the end of the day, I think, Sid was pragmatic enough to say that everybody's going to have to compromise, both sides are going to have to compromise; and it's my view that nothing ever gets done unless there is compromise on both sides. The problem today is that compromise is considered weak, and particularly for Republicans, they don't want to be perceived as compromising," he adds.

Throughout his career, Devaney looked back at the advice he received from Professor Wise. "I think that the connection between myself and Sid is in the way he taught and the way he approached government studies," he said. "I've had countless offers at countless salaries that made my wife cry when I went home and told her I'm not doing it. 'Well, why aren't we doing it?' Because I like what I'm doing, I can effect change, I can do what I like to do, I can do important things and effect change, particularly at this job, given the state of the economy and what's going on, it's probably a pretty important role. I wouldn't walk away from something like that, no matter what the money was. I just never felt like leaving government. It's not patriotism per se, it's just the way I think F&M shaped me in thinking about government service being a noble thing, and it was a tremendous effect on me. I'm not the most famous of all his kids, but nonetheless, he had a big influence on me."

Wise's influence on Devaney began early and never waned. "You sat there [as a student] listening, riveted to what he was doing, and you knew he was only talking about theory, but he understood the government and how it worked," he recalls. "I had three-and-a-half years at F&M, but it was a great three-and-a-half years, and I loved Lancaster."

There were other lessons that shaped Devaney's perspective, and led to his role as one of the government's most effective anti-corruption watchdogs. "Integrity, that's another lesson I took away from my whole F&M experience, but certainly within the government department, I think they always preached that. Law enforcement, particularly in the early-'70s when I started my career, was a pretty no-nonsense profession, and I never fit in to that. I was always sort of out of the box, I could see the benefit of giving somebody a second chance. I wasn't particularly a death penalty advocate. So I found myself a little bit estranged from my fellow law enforcement folks when I was first in the Secret Service, probably on the more liberal end of the thing, and I think that came from my experience at F&M," Devaney notes. "So I was always sort of an odd duck in law enforcement, and may have benefited from that because it came to the attention of leadership as being not your average sheep in the herd, but somebody a little different and people want to listen to what he has to say. So I think I got that from F&M, I think I got that from Sid."

"In the Secret Service, you serve the President and the Vice-President in very non-political way," he explains. "If the President changes tomorrow, you don't change your job. I think whether it's a Democratic President or Republican President, you're still going to do your utmost to protect them. I knew after I got into law enforcement that I wanted to be as non-political as I possibly could be in a career, and never aspired to hold appointed office to any particular party, because you know, at the end of the day, you're out, and then I didn't want to leave government. So I stayed in the Secret Service, and then went over to EPA. I first served a Republic administration and Carol Browner came in, for eight years. Clinton appointed me to the Interior Department as IG, on the basis of non-political appointments; they're appointed supposedly on the basis of their professional backgrounds. So they never asked me when they went to appoint me whether I was a Democrat or Republican."

Becoming the point man against fraud in the Stimulus Program was yet another step forward, albeit one with some family implications as well. "I'm on a leave of absence, and I got a call one day from the Vice President who said, 'I'd like to talk to you about something, can you come over Monday? The President and I would like to make you the Chairman of this Board, we'd like to talk Monday a little bit more about it, why don't you think about it over the weekend.' Now here's where I made the biggest mistake of my life: I did not mention to my wife that I was going to do this on Monday."

"So Monday comes, I go over to the White House, and I speak to the Vice President, and I had practiced all weekend how to say no to a Vice President, because my wife and I had were having discussions about retirement, where we're going to live, what are we going to do, it's my 40th year, wouldn't it be nice to make it 40 and go, we don't have money issues, we can do this, go to Florida or Cape Cod," Devaney says. "So I hadn't said anything to my wife, and now I'm sitting in front of the Vice President, and I had practiced how to say no to a Vice President, and I'm sort of hedging a little bit, and he's telling me what his perception of this is, and I ask him a couple of questions that I thought might be deal killers and they weren't."

The next thing Devaney knew he was with President Obama. "So [Vice President Biden] said, 'Well, let's go see the President'. 'Let's go see the President? 'Yeah.' So we get up, walk in, see the President. 'Well, you're going to take the job, right?' [Obama asked.] And then I said okay; he said, 'Do you have any questions?'; I said, 'Yes, Mr. President, when would you make this announcement?' He said, 'In 10 minutes.' So I walked with him down to the National Governor's Conference, which was in the Roosevelt Room, the Red Room, and he announced it. Now, my wife hears from a colleague at work that I've just been on CNN being announced as the new Chairman of this Board, and have made a four-and-a-half year commitment to the President. Let me put it this way: Mother's Day was very expensive for me this year. So that's my story. It was unexpected. I had been preaching for years, all my career, about transparency and accountability, and this is probably the grandest experience in transparency and accountability ever. So can you put up for the American people to see, for the very first time, how their money is actually being spent; preventing fraud and waste of such an enormous amount of money is another challenge – so there's two sets of challenges here, one that I just couldn't walk away from," Devaney notes.

The President did not ask about Devaney's political affiliations. "I'd been serving over there for 10 years, and when President Obama and I ended up in the Oval Office with him, he didn't ask me if I was a Republican or Democrat," Devaney recalls. "I don't think he assumed either one, he was just looking for somebody with the right credentials for this job. As much as people would like to paint me into certain corners because I was appointed by Clinton, Obama has given me this job. As much as the people who don't like the recovery plan up on the Hill would like to paint me as something other than non-partisan, I've been able to maintain that thing, and that's a difficult thing to maintain for 40 years."

No matter what the position, Devaney stayed in touch with Professor Wise. "I would periodically drop Sid a line, tell him that I'd just been promoted, I was in Los Angeles, or whatever; and he, in turn, if he saw something in the paper, would drop me a line," he recalls, "I think when I went to EPA as director over there, he sent me a note congratulating me and inviting me to come up. As my name would come to his attention as I moved through government into different positions and all the way out, I would get an occasional phone call or note from Sid."

Devaney also hired interns who were directed to him by Professor Wise. "He had sent a couple of students to me in the EPA," he notes. "I hired them as summer interns. He was always looking for those opportunities. The summer intern thing for credit or for money was never a problem, I could do that all I wanted."

It was learning government, not political science, at F&M that stayed with Devaney. "Sometimes when I say to people what I majored in, I always say government. 'You mean political science?' [they ask.] I said, 'No, government, the governing piece there. I love that about F&M, I would say that 90% of people who actually majored in something to do with their job in government call it political science. "The inspiration came from Sid Wise. Sid had the classroom on the right-hand side in the front, and the windows would always be wide open," Devaney recalls. "If you weren't taking a class with him and you were walking by, you'd hear him, and look in and smile, and go to the library or coffee shop. It was kind of a clubby thing, the government department." In the end, Devaney became a member of another club, one whose members helped change life in Washington by assuring that there was a place for honesty in government service.

# Dan Cohen – Mr. Film

When most people think of Sid Wise, they remember him as a professor or mentor; others recall him just as vividly for his love of cinema, and his role creating and managing the College Film Series. To alumni and colleagues, the Film Series was a weekly event in which the College showed a wide range of movies, from current features to foreign films to the types of films shown at festivals. Regardless, for many students, the Film Series provided one of the few forms of entertainment and diversion on the campus. Interestingly, virtually every time the Film Series is mentioned, Dan Cohen's name immediately pops up. Cohen, a 1971 graduate of the College who now lives in California, was close to Sid Wise both as a student and after graduation. He also wrote many of the movie reviews/previews that would appear in *The College Reporter.*

Originally from Lancaster, Cohen has written and directed three independent feature films, including the award winning *Diamond Men,* which film critic Roger Ebert called "a treasure." Cohen believes "that without [his] relationship with [Sid, he] would have never become a film maker because there wasn't even a film class. He was the one who developed that, and we talked about that endlessly because while we basically lived in Lancaster our heads were in this nutty art form. Sidney used to say, 'My job is to disappoint a different 20 percent of the audience each week [for the film series].' [When] we started out there would be 80 people in the audience, and then later on we had to show [a movie] two times and it's four hours, each piece of it [per weekend]. We had to put rows of chairs in the back – 500-600 people [to accommodate the demand]."

Cohen "worked hand in hand with Sid from the time [he] was 18 until [his] early forties." The pair had a mutual love of film, government and public policy. "Neither of us had a clue about the actual making of films, but we were desperately interested in everything, watching them, reading about them, following them from an aesthetic point of view; what makes them good, what makes them bad. We both had an urgent need to devour movies; read about them, read all the books. Of course, there was a time until I was in college where it was possible for a person to consume all the important literature that was written about film. You would start with somebody like Eisenstein, who was a theorist, and work up to Siegfried Kracauer, and then go to the people who wrote about the lively arts. Then there was an explosion of PhDs in the 60s and the 70s that made it impossible – when the proliferation of film as an academic study after the new wave and the auteur theory came into being – making it impossible to read everything out there.

Cohen recalls Wise as "the consummate community politician. He was on this College Senate part of the time I was there. Sid's thing was public policy; that's the art of compromise. He taught me the Socratic method, and [I learned how to] listen to a position [I] vehemently disagreed with, and then somehow function within the confines of that and sort of beat it out. But in the same token, [Sid would show how to] do it without resorting to bullying. There is an art to politics and that is the maneuvering within a set of people; it is also when to hold back and who to talk to. You had to respect [Sid and his colleagues'] ability to handle these difficult situations with an air of civility."

"Sidney taught the Socratic Method; he came in and started asking questions, he was brilliant at drawing you into knowledge. The first thing I remember him teaching in class was that people – after '68 or '69, with the war and so forth – had a natural aversion to politics. They viewed politics as the enemy of progress of humankind, but Sid the first day of class would say, 'What exactly is politics? It's the interaction of two people, to begin with. If you don't like politics you obviously can't talk to anybody because people are always behaving in a political fashion.' It was rather simple but it profoundly set you on your ear because you really had to rethink everything you thought you knew about. He said, 'This is an experiment; it's an experiment that was started in 1776 and it evolves as an experiment,' and then really set you to thinking. You had a tremendous respect for him for the way he opened your eyes. Sydney had a didactic impulse."

# Joseph Karlesky – "He Brought Me Sheets"

The Honorable and Mrs. John C. Kunkel Professor of Government at F&M, and the Provost of the College, Joe Karlesky was a colleague of Sid Wise's for decades. Yet it is Sid Wise's simple kindnesses that have made the most lasting imprint on Professor Karlesky.

"From practically the first moment I arrived on campus, he showed me kindness which I will never forget. I came to Lancaster and had nothing except clothes and books. When I moved to Lancaster there were two memories of Sidney that are absolutely indelible to me. Sidney was very gracious in asking me if I needed anything. It turns out I didn't have any bed sheets, and he and Eileen gave me bed sheets. Now that's a very tiny, simple thing, but you can't imagine how much that meant to me," he recalls. "The other early incident that I recall is that since I did not have a car, [Sid] took me to Jay's Supermarket. I vividly remember him taking me there and while I went around putting cans of tomato soup in the basket, Sidney very kindly and patiently waited at the front of the store, and we packed up and he took me to the place I was living. He was a genuine nurturer and a mentor. He seemed to get his reasons for living out of doing that, and that suffused his teaching, it suffused his relationship with students, it suffused his relationships with alumni. You just don't find people like that anymore on campuses. But he was your classic community rock."

Like other colleagues, Karlesky believes that Wise's impact on the College was as significant as it was on numerous students. "What we should all think about is what kind of place this would have been without people like him, and what kind of place do we risk without having people like him. And how much he enriched the place when he was here, and what the absence of that kind of enrichment means to the kind of place we are now. Well, you teach it by example, and you also teach it by informal discussions."

"One of the things [Sid] taught me is that you be kind to people who are at a lower status than you are. You appreciate all of the contributions throughout the campus. In addition, Sid, [John Vanderzell and Dick Schier] encouraged us to retain relationships with alumni because we saw them do it."

"Sidney, for as long as I remember, was the sole creator and contributor to the department's career conference. Every year, he would contact four people, ask them to come in on an evening or late afternoon to talk about how they got to where they are. It's a tradition that's as old as I remember and it continues. That was Sidney's idea, it was his baby. It was his creature, and it kind of symbolized helping current students by drawing on the knowledge and successes of alumni. He was very big on I'm going to help you do X, but don't forget that when you're in a position to help Y, you help Y. It was kind of that. It's part of that nurturing process. I don't know how different I would be as a professor if I came either at a different time, or in a department that didn't have [Professors Wise, Schier and Vanderzell]."

"What has always struck me is that on this campus and probably others as well, there is a kind of a periodic discussion about how do we enrich community, how do we strengthen community, and how do we get to be a better community. It's all wheel spinning. Sidney did it before people talked about it as a problem. He just simply did it, and it was people like him who just made it the kind of place it was. There's no way to know how to bottle what Sidney did and said, institutionalizing, because he kind of just gave totally of himself."

Karlesky also notes the impact of the troika of Professors Wise, Vanderzell and Schier. "They developed a lot of good relationships with students, and they were relationships that lasted. They did the mentoring, and then it was like a departmental norm, a departmental tradition. It was just the sort of thing that you did. I mean you would never think of not going to the homecoming event. I mean that was just simply unthinkable. There was just kind of an expectation that, of course you would talk to alumni. So there is a lot of what Sidney did that is genuinely unique in that he could be a teacher of us, and he could give us examples, but there was no way that I – that any of us – could really replicate that."

Despite their desire to encourage students to enter public service, the professors eschewed partisan politics in those dealings. "Nobody who knew Sidney was unaware that this guy was a Capitol Hill Democrat, but that did not influence his relationships with his students. He could get along with Duberstein and encourage him in his career because Sidney above everything else had a tremendous respect for the process. He was one of those old time pols, and it's the process that counts, that we're not going to get everything that we want, but if we persist in trying to get that which others want to deny us, and if we just keep persisting then the whole process is going to collapse. He was a real defender of the political process, and as a result of that he was able to be sensitive to all manner of ideologies and conflicts. I think that really infused his teaching. Students appreciated that politics is an honorable profession."

Wise also could pinpoint those students with potential to make a difference. "He had a capacity. He could see a spark. He could see people and make comments about them that were just right on the mark. He saw it as part of his life's calling, trying to encourage people to be interested in politics, to live to their fullest potential. At the same time, he was just a very smart guy and he could see things in people that the rest of us probably didn't."

That insight helped other faculty members reach their potential. "As a young faculty member, he was terrific because he taught me how to negotiate the place, what's important, what to do, what not to do, but at the same time very sensitive and receptive to the way I wanted to teach courses and so forth. I couldn't possibly ask for someone who was kinder to me, and I just don't know where I would have ended up if I had a different kind of departmental context. In his prime, he was a real mover on campus."

"His personality was very warm, open, and generous. He was always looking out for what would help the college, what would help X, and what would help Y. I never got the sense of "*How this is going to help me.*" He was a terrific advisor because of that kind of openness and nurturing that he had with just about everybody that he met."

In addition, Karlesky notes the impact of the film series that Wise oversaw. "Sid, more than any other person on campus, was responsible for the Franklin Schaffner Film Library. The premiere of *Boys from Brazil* was held on campus, it was just a major coup for the college to have something like that."

"There are people that go through your life that you were just lucky to have known them, and he was one in my life. I was just lucky to have known him, and to watch him do what he did. I was just very fortunate in seeing it," Karlesky recalls.

# D. Brooks Smith – Gentleness Is Exactly What We Need Right Now

Judge D. Brooks Smith sits on the United States Court of Appeals for the Third Circuit, to which he was nominated in September of 2001. He previously served on the United States District Court for the Western District of Pennsylvania from 1988 until his confirmation in 2002, serving as the Chief Judge from 2001 until his elevation to the Third Circuit. As a judge on the Third Circuit, he hears appeals from Federal cases arising in Pennsylvania, New Jersey, Delaware and the U.S. Virgin Islands. Judge Smith received his bachelor's degree from F&M in 1973, and his law degree from the Dickinson School of Law in 1976. He served as Blair County District Attorney and was subsequently appointed to and then elected to the Court of Common Pleas of Blair County, eventually becoming the court's Administrative Judge. Judge Smith has also authored numerous articles and serves on many committees. He also has assisted in efforts to enhance the rule of law in the judicial systems of Central and Eastern Europe and has taught judicial training sessions in Russia for the Department of State and, with the American Bar Association's Central and Eastern European Legal Initiative in Bulgaria, Latvia and Albania with the United States Agency for International Development (USAID); in Kosovo, with the International Development Law Organization; and in Bosnia and Macedonia with the U.S. Justice Department's Office of Overseas Prosecutorial Development, Assistance and Training.

As is common, judicial nominations can be politically charged. Judge Smith's nomination to the 3rd Circuit Court of Appeals was highly contentious, with

*The New York Times* opposing his nomination in its lead editorial because of the judge's strong conservative views. Despite vocal opposition, Judge Smith's nomination was approved and he continues to serve with distinction on the Court. When he looks back at the influences in his life, Professor Wise is at the top of the list.

Judge Smith enrolled at F&M in 1969 "with an interest in government, with an interest in political science. Strangely though, at the time I was also considering divinity school. It turned out to be a damn good thing for both the church and me, I think, that I re-thought that thing and ended up a government major with a pretty significant concentration in economics. But needless to say, in a small school, all departments are relatively small, you got to know Sid Wise. The names Wise and Schier were always connected as well. I took Sidney's course on political parties I believe. I took a number of his courses."

"He was always Professor Wise, Doctor Wise," Judge Smith recalls. "And at the same time, his accessibility [was] his personal interest that he took in really just about anybody who wanted his personal interest. That was the great generosity of the man I think. It wasn't because he spotted you either as a candidate for a PhD or as most definitely a Phi Beta Kappa. He was receptive, accessible and interesting."

Judge Smith recalled that Professors Wise and Schier took an interest in their students' political activities, regardless of their party affiliation. "I remember [Sid] as having an interest in everybody's political activity, and his student's political activity," he says. "I come from a county, and still live there, where

Republicans dominate and always have. He and Schier were definitely old leftists in their politics, and nevertheless had a keen interest in what anybody was doing, or whatever their political bent was if they were students, and what particular political efforts they got involved in."

"[The Vietnam War] was no impediment at all to his interest in me and in other students. I remember him, as well as Professor Schier, in the years I was there, which were from the fall of '69 to my graduation in the spring of '73. These were Vietnam War years. These were tough years on a campus. And the interesting ideological shift, political shift if you will, was to see two members of the professoriate, who were definitely historically blue blood by Lancaster County standards, become viewed by a lot of students as reactionary," he notes.

"These guys were traditionalist when it came to education pedagogy. They did not react – Schier was much less polite about it, Sidney was always his low-key very diplomatic self. But the notion that students could just shut-down classes and show up for classes any time they damn-well pleased, was really not part of their pedagogy, their approach to higher education. And so much of that was fed by just the bad spirit that existed on campuses, including F&M, as a result of the reaction to Vietnam War opposition."

"I watched the reaction of Sidney to so much of the anti-war movement on the educational process and the degree of severity it was on the campus, and it clearly disturbed him. He would talk about it in class," Smith recalls. "I look back and there were the areas of concentration academically within the political science field, and law and law school were not the areas of interest that he would have had. He was a political parties guy, a legislative process guy."

"Recalling the experience of being in his class and being subject to his pedagogical approach, I'm sure I learned much about teaching. I'm an adjunct and have been now for a number of years at Penn State Dickinson [School of Law]. His teaching approach, while of considerable academic rigor, was also to be very anecdotal, using the ability to teach through human example and anecdotes. This is a wonderful thing to witness, and it's a great thing to learn. If you're going to teach yourself – if you're going to give a speech, even if you're going to relate to people on a one-to-one basis, the ability to do it through concrete examples with human experience, stories, anecdotes, teaches us more often than we realize at the time we hear them. His teaching approach encompassed a lot of that.

Equally important, Judge Smith remembers that Professor Wise's "words were carefully chosen, and he used them as weapons." In addition, Professor Wise stayed in touch with his former student. "I actually was the district attorney for a year in my county. I was an assistant DA and I spent a few years there as a special prosecutor working on an investigative grand jury, organized crime detail. My career path was not in partisan politics. If anything, I ended up avoiding it."

"What I remember and what I was taught, and what was been of use to me from both his course content and his pedagogy, was characterized by such gentleness. But at the same time, we know he was no easy touch. The life lesson that Sidney imparted through that teaching, and that pedagogy is exactly what we need right now. That he would have had an interest in an equal number of Republican students to the Democratic members of the F&M community is a testament to the values he had as a human being, and what he understood about a diverse society. It needs civil discourse, and he did it in a time when we weren't even talking about diversity the way we do now."

"I could just imagine Sidney shaking his head at the politics that we've seen since his death. It really got especially bad during the Clinton years with impeachment – for both sides it's been nothing but gotcha politics over the last many years."

Of note, Judge Smith pondered what his mentor's reaction would have been to his own nomination. "I have no doubt that [Sid] would have been energized by my own antagonists while going through Senate confirmation in 2002, because I had the bad fortune of [being] the object of the lead editorial one day in the *New York Times*. And *The Times* was the Bible of Sidney. I mean I can still remember him walking from his house with his little cigar and the *New York Times* often under his arm as he'd walk from Race Avenue up to Old Main. He would have wanted to get involved, I have no doubt. He would have made a few phone calls to try to help."

When Professor Wise retired from teaching, he joined the College's Development (fund raising) office. "The college was wise enough, no pun intended, to enlist Sidney to contact certain people to make contributions," notes Judge Smith. "I've never made a lot of money, but only Sidney would have been able to probably talk me into the increase in the contribution I made from being left to my own devices to his direct contact. They were so smart to tap into his goodwill. It was good of him to do that, because that was really not the kind of thing that Sidney did. He loved the college."

"I remember him as being such a very important part of the identity of Franklin and Marshall at that time. He was such a pillar. He was an influence within academic politics. He was a force to be reckoned with there."

# Darrell Dwyer '71

A friend of mine, William Abnett, and I were taking Dr. Wise's Introduction to Government class and were quite late to class, having spent too much time partying the night before. The class was set up with the lectern in front of the door so the lecturer's back was also to the door. We literally stumbled into the class, I believe knocking over a chair in the process.

Finding our seats and looking up, we saw George McGovern was the unannounced guest speaker for that day! Dr. Wise saved his reprimand for the next class where he proclaimed, "Gentlemen [we were yet to be coed at this time], in the future if you are going to be more than ten minutes late to my class please don't bother to come!"

# John Martino – The Value of a Phone Call

John Martino, a Lancaster native, graduated as a government major in 1974. Following graduation, he held a variety of posts, including serving as an Assistant to Congressman Robert S. Walker from 1977 to 1979. After serving the Congressman, Mr. Martino because the Executive Assistant to the Secretary of the Commonwealth of Pennsylvania, then was promoted to Deputy Secretary of the Commonwealth, and Deputy Secretary of the Department of Community Affairs. He left government service, and operated his own business, Keystone Data, before being nominated by President George W. Bush as Director of the U.S. Mint, a position he would hold from 1989 to 1993.

As a student, Martino embraced the Government Department's teaching philosophy. "I always hearken back to Sid and Dick Schier, teaching moderate politics, 'the center,' [that] we were a centrist society fundamentally. If you go too far to the right and you go too far to the left you go into the gutters," he notes. "They extolled upon us to keep that in mind, and always kept me on a moderate course. When I was County [Republican] Chairman, I think it served me well."

Martino also learned that government is local. "Government is not all at the Federal level," he says. "If you want to make an impact, don't shy away from getting involved in local government or state government. It's a disservice to our society if you think that the Federal Government can solve every [or] inject itself into every problem."

Like other alumni, John Martino knew Sid Wise when he was a student, but got to know him even better after graduation. "Where I really got to know [Sid], however, was when I graduated. I stayed on campus as the Assistant Alumni Director. It was during that time where I got to know Sid very well.

"[Sid] was a great alumni draw. People would come back to see Professor Wise," Martino explains. "It wasn't so much the subject matter. People would come back and say, 'We're just happy to be here and see him and chat with him.'" Part of Dr. Wise's "draw" was his connections and his ability to help alumni network. "We also had a program called: "Is There Life After F&M?" We would bring back alumni who had careers in Government – we'd have a full house. There's nothing like being a student and saying, 'Hey, the people who went ahead of me seem to do pretty well. They have interesting jobs and they're willing to come back and talk to us.' Sid was very helpful in making that happen."

Martino also relied on Sid for career advice and entrees into government positions. "I wanted to expand my horizons a little bit. I wanted to look at state government, for example, and [Richard] Thornburg had been elected Governor. Again, keeping Sid apprised of my career developments was [critical]. He'd say to me, 'Do you know Ken Duberstein?' I'd say, 'Well I certainly know *of* him. Ken was class of like '66.' And Sid said, 'You know, you and he are on similar progressions in that you both worked for the college right after you graduated. Let me call Ken Duberstein.' This is [around] '79. He picked up the phone, called Ken. He said, 'Hey Ken, I don't know if you know anybody in the Thornburg camp, but if you do I have a really good guy here that's trying to get in with them.' Sure enough

147

within two weeks, I got a call for an interview. I was hired in the Department of Community Affairs as Special Assistant to the Secretary. I wound up staying where I was and became Deputy Secretary within a year or so. During that time I got involved as a Republican Committeeman in the precinct that F&M is in."

Shortly after George Bush's election, "[Martino] got a call from the Washington White House, in their HR Department. They said, 'Would you be interested in joining the Administration?' I said, 'If you could find something in Pennsylvania, I'll consider it.' I thought, I'll never hear from them. About three weeks later, they called up and said, 'Would you be interested in running the United States Mint in Philadelphia?' You know, I never thought of it," he remembers. "So, I called Sid, and I said, 'Sid, what do you think?' He said, 'Well you know John, I hadn't given a lot of thought to it, but let me ponder it, you know you're going to be running a factory. That's what [the Mint] is. It's 24 hours a day, it's a factory.'"

Under Federal law[6], the President appoints the Director of the United States Mint; the appointment requires approval of the U.S. Senate following a hearing before and vote by the Committee on Banking. At the time, because of political squabbles, the Democratically-controlled Senate was not holding hearings or approving any nominations from the Republican President. Of course, the nomination of Mr. Martino, a former Chair of the Lancaster County Republican Party, was precisely the type of selection the Democratic Senate was opposing. But on October 8, 1989, the

---

[6] 31 USC § 304

Senate confirmed Mr. Martino to be Superintendent of the Mint of the United States at Philadelphia without the requisite hearing. How? Sid Wise made a phone call.

After agreeing to accept the position, Martino recalled all the hoops that he had to jump through. "The Bush Administration required a full background check before they named you. The full background check is very exhausting. They tell you right up front that you have to fill out an application that's not an application, it's a profile for the FBI. Then the FBI shows up at your house for a detailed interview."

"The White House said, you really should be divesting yourself of your personal business because we don't want that business – unless you put it in a sophisticated escrow account. I'm just a middle class guy trying to make a living, I have a family to support. So, I had to go and give up my consulting business."

"Here is where it gets interesting. There were two newspapers in Lancaster County, *The [Intelligencer-Journal]* and the *New Era*. One was profoundly Republican and the other was profoundly Democratic. At any rate, the Bush people insisted that before they name people, they had to complete the background investigation. That took a couple of months. I'm sitting there. I'm divesting myself of the business. I'm going into a business cocoon. I'm on the phone with Sid saying, 'you know, this is kind of an inside story of the sacrifice you make if you're going to be an appointee. You have to close down your business. You're still kind of on tender hooks because you don't know if they're going to come back and say sorry something came up in your background that we're not going to appoint.'"

"Eventually, the appointment comes out. Bush makes a series of announcements. I was probably one of 30 that day. Of course a local paper picks it up. *The Intel* had the first scoop on it. They did the story and then the very next day, they had an editorial. In the editorial they said, hey John Martino is a good guy, he deserves something in the White House, maybe in the political arm. But, he was Party Chairman. Why would he be qualified to run the Mint? It was an editorial, and it was very hurtful because I had never met the editors. I had never met anybody."

"The next day there is a letter from Sid in the paper, saying John Martino has a mountain of integrity and let's end this debate. Let's just talk about the importance of having people as appointees. Good people, honest people, hardworking people, they don't have to have expertise in a specific field as long as they are good generalists and he's one of them. It shut down the entire debate in its entirety. There was no partisanship after that. It shut the debate off in the community. There was no debate. It was like they came out with an editorial, Sid's letter came out, and it was gone, everything was quiet. I was forever grateful. It was unrequested. It came out the next day. He moved so quickly and shut down any contentious debate."

"Then the next big pivot was once I was publicly appointed, the nomination had to go to the Senate. In those days, Congress was controlled by the Democrats. Obviously, the White House was Republican, right. My nomination had to go over and it had to go to the Banking Committee. I was told, it's being sent over. You wait around for a few weeks, and meanwhile – I had already been waiting for months anyway with the background check going on, I was divesting myself. I was sitting there saying, 'gee, I'm a middle class kid here, I don't have money to live off of. I have to support my family. I was also keeping in touch with Sid because of the academic side of the Senate confirmation, I had never been through it before."

"One day I went over in some mild frustration because I received a call from the FBI saying that they wanted to talk to me. Something came up in my background check. They wanted to know why I had a protracted bout with mononucleosis when I was 33 years old. I was somewhat frustrated and said, if that's the worst they can ask me about, I'm okay with that, but it is frustrating."

Meanwhile, the Senate still said we are not processing any nominees in the Senate because we want to see the raw data in all the background checks. It has nothing to do with anybody personally; we want to see the pure raw data file from the FBI field background."

"The Bush people said, 'hey guys, you've taken it out of context. You could really kill people with that. This is raw interview data. Negative comments are written down verbatim, positives are simply summarized because they expect to get positives.' That was the face-off. So here we are at a stalemate, but I'm not working. You know. It's now heading into October and this has been in the wind since January or February at the latest.

"I went to see Sid and we talked. He said, 'you know what John, I think we may have an alum who works on the Hill, let me give her a call.' It was a woman from the Class of '76. He called her and said, do you

151

know John Martino? You may know him, he's a sweetheart of a guy. She said, 'you know what, my husband works on that committee. He's the Chief Counsel of the Banking Committee.' I think the way it went was like this. Steve [Harris] called me. I then made an appointment to go down and see him. This was all happening within a week."

"I'm sitting there for seven or eight months without a paycheck, not being processed and getting frustrated and Sid makes this one phone call and I'm in a car down to Washington literally within a week. I sat down with Steve Harris, who's a wonderful nice guy. I had done some reading on the Mint and Steve said to me, 'What does the Superintendent do?' And I said, from what I know, this is what they do. Boom, boom, boom. This is the oversight area that they have. This is the organizational chart. This is the location, obviously in Philadelphia. He said, okay, but didn't say anything more. We had a very nice chat. We ended it. A week later I got notice in the mail that my hearing was waived, which the Senate can do. They can waive the hearing."

"Much to the surprise of everybody – I never told people in Washington how I thought this came about. They said, that's great, we don't know why, but a little bit of the logjam broke in your case, and don't argue with the umpire. I said, that's great with me. Senate confirmation took place. I was sworn in in mid-October of 1989. That really was a Sid Wise phone call. Again, that broke a deadlock between the legislature and the White House."

With President Bush seeking re-election, Martino was concerned about the outcome and again consulted his former professors. "I had a real good instinctive feeling. I remember at the time saying to people, Bush's approval rating of 92 percent after the first Iraq war isn't going to last. I had a real uneasy feeling about the election. I started banking my vacation and sick time and decided to go to pick up my graduate degree. I counseled with Sid very briefly. Sid just said getting a Master's Degree is a good move for you. Joe Karlesky was also very helpful in pointing me in the right direction. [As a result,] I picked up my Master's Degree in Public Administration."

Martino believes that there remains a place in government for moderates. "I honestly think there are a lot of good guys – Ken Duberstein showed where you can be politically active and can also be in government. Sometimes we deny that. Sometimes it gets partisan. Maybe we're not doing the proper education in our systems where we talk about that. But, you can be a good politician and also a good governor. I mean governor in the small 'g' or administrator."

Martino hopes that more centrists can be attracted to government positions. "One of the things that the F&M people were very good about was that they taught how a careerist and the appointee can work together. What's the accommodation? How do you gain each other's respect?"

No matter where he was, Martino recalled Sid Wise's advice, and his desire for civility rather than the combative nature so common in current political discourse. "I think the perspective that Sid and Dick Schier would apply is that there's always been some contact aspect of politics. You have to expect that it's a contact sport. Some of that perspective would be there, but I think they would be disappointed with the lack of collegiality, the lack of a consistent sort of civilized tone today. I think they valued that very much. The ability to be friends with people behind the scenes, to have a legitimate debate, and not poke at someone because of their political beliefs. We need to respect the fact that we have two parties, and that both parties have contributed quantumly to our success."

# Debra Amper-Kahn – People Are the Core of Politics

Debra Amper-Kahn "came to F&M for its radio station and to avoid Physical Education. But [she] stayed and thrived because of Sid Wise." Since graduating from F&M in 1975 *cum laude* and Phi Beta Kappa, earning a M.A. from the Eagleton Institute of Politics at Rutgers University, Amper-Kahn has devoted her life to improving public education, to philanthropy, and to community affairs. Currently, the Executive Director of Delaware Valley Grantmakers, she served as the City of Philadelphia Secretary of Education from 2000 to 2005, was a member of the Philadelphia School Board, and serves on the Boards of numerous community-based organizations.

When she came to F&M, Amper-Kahn had no idea what career to pursue. She met Professor Wise, but doesn't remember when or why. "I think one of the many wonderful things about Sid, which I think you could say about most people who are sort of mentors, is that they know you better than you know yourself, and that's particularly true of an 18 year old; they see something in you that you don't see in yourself."

Amper-Kahn recalls F&M as "such a welcoming place and I think its distinctive feature is the relationships that students have with faculty, including Sid Wise. He was, of course, so engaging. He also had a great way of relating to parents. He did wonderful things for me." She recalls taking a course in "Public Opinion" with Professor Wise. "It was the spring semester, so I remember being home [after the semester ended] and the phone rang, and I was a little concerned because I ran out of time when I took the exam, because I had so much to write in the blue book.

"I remember my mother coming in to tell me, 'Mr. Wise is on the phone.' 'Oh my God. I really bombed this thing. He's going to tell me, right,'" she thought. "I stumbled to the phone and I'm like, I'm really sorry. I know I ran out of time and you know I know the stuff. He said, 'that's not why I'm calling.' And he was offering me this incredible opportunity. That year Ben Bradlee was the graduation speaker. He offered me the opportunity to go to Washington and escort him in the car driving Ben Bradlee and Sally Quinn from Washington.

"It was, I remind you, during the height of Watergate. He was the graduation speaker. It was a once in a lifetime opportunity," she recalls. Professor Wise's influence continued. He was "also responsible for where [she] went to graduate school, because [she] had no clue what [she] was going to do."

During her senior year, Amper-Kahn "had applied to all journalism programs. One day I get this note in my mailbox [asking me to see Professor Wise]. So I came to see him. And he had this literature from the Eagleton Institute of Politics, he sort of threw it at me. He said, 'Take a look at this.' And I said, 'sounds good for somebody.' He said, 'you, stupid,' basically. And I went, 'oh.' He said, 'Look. It's right here where you grew up. Just check it out when you go home and then do whatever. Amper-Kahn visited the school over the ensuing Christmas break, and went there for graduate school, and that experience has led to Amper-Kahn's career in education and public service, a career inspired by Professor Wise and Professor Schier.

Amper-Kahn notes that her education in the Government Department has been a mainstay in her career. "It was the theory in action, and the theory in practice, but there were always people at the core and at the center, whether they were the practitioners or the citizens. The message, the lesson from F&M is that one without the other, it just doesn't work. You had to keep that humanity at the core." To this day, she still thinks about Professor Wise. "They're always sort of back there somewhere, almost watching over [me]. Sometimes it's the what would Sid do question [that I ask myself]." When she became a member of the Philadelphia School Board, Sid came to her swearing in. "There it was, public service. There was a certain pride that I knew that he would feel a certain confidence that I would do good, even if it was hard, and do well. In addition, there's a set of values and principles that they conveyed [at F&M], in addition to the education, which was the ability to think.

"It wasn't just about inspiration at the college. The point was you had to think, and you had to come up with your arguments and you had to be able to express them to a very high standard. And that is a gift and a legacy that I know I take with me, having those kinds of high standards. So I think it's the combination of the principles, the values, the skills and some of the content that, I think it's what propelled us [after graduation]."

# Maria Falco – He Took Everyone Seriously

Maria Falco never attended F&M, nor did she ever work with Sid. Dr. Falco, a Fulbright Scholar who received her Ph.D. in Political Science from Bryn Mawr College, recalls Sid Wise for the support he provided at the outset of her academic career, when women were often not taken seriously.

"I was teaching American Government at Immaculata College while Sid was at Franklin and Marshall. I moved to Washington College in Chestertown, Maryland. While there, Sid recommended I interview for one of the faculty fellowships in state and local politics being offered by the National Center for Education Politics. My application was approved. I was awarded a fellowship to serve as Genevieve Blatt's research assistant, while she ran for the U.S. Senate against Hugh Scott." After the election, Falco "wrote a book about the election, *"Bigotry!:" Ethnic, Machine, Sexual Politics in the Senatorial Election,* but because few publishers were interested in women in politics at the time, it did not get published until 1980."

She recalls Wise's help with an earlier book. In 1973, she published *Truth and Meaning in Political Science: An Introduction to Political Inquiry,* and "was invited to participate in the [American Political Science Association's] conference on the small college at French Lick, Indiana. While there, Sid Wise praised [her] new book to the entire membership. In fact, he held it up at the conference. As a result, Austin Ranney, the incoming president of the APSA invited [her] to chair an entire section, seven panels of the 1975 APSA convention program on epistemology and methodology. [She] later gathered all the panel papers and as many of the discussions as possible and published them in a book, *Through the Looking-Glass: Epistemology and the Conduct of Political Inquiry: an Anthology.*"

"In short," recalls Falco, "at very critical moments in my career Sid Wise drew attention to my abilities at a time when few women were even noticed in academia. He took every chance he got to advance somebody else's agenda, and not just his own, and helped me at a time when nobody was paying attention to women."

# Paula Dow – "I'm the new continuing process of the great founding fathers who made America great"

Paula Dow grew up in Yeadon, a small town outside of Philadelphia, and then found herself, an African-American woman, at a newly coed school in Lancaster, a city known for farms and cows. From that unlikely beginning, Paula Dow's career began. As a freshman, her roommate was Mary Schapiro, who would become Chair of the Securities and Exchange Commission under President Barrack Obama. Dow set out on her own direction after graduating from F&M in 1977 as a dual Economics and Government major. She then graduated from the University of Pennsylvania Law School in 1980 and went to work for Exxon. Her first exposure to public service came in 1987 when she served as a Deputy U.S. Attorney under U.S. Attorney Rudolph Giuliani. She next joined the office of the United States Attorney for the District of New Jersey, and served as Counsel to U.S. Attorney Chris Christie from 2002 to 2003. From 2003 to 2009, she served as Essex County (N.J.) Prosecutor, and was appointed as New Jersey Attorney General in 2009 by Governor Christie, the first African-American woman to hold the position. In 2012, the New Jersey Senate approved her nomination as a Superior Court Judge in Burlington County.

Dow came to F&M because her high school guidance counselor told her that the college was seeking to diversify more. "So one day [she] got on the train, went to Lancaster, saw this hokey town – I saw the cows. I remember to this day, looking at, and thinking how can I tell my classmates this is the kind of setting that I'm going to spend the next four years, when everyone was still – '73 was still really active, in the civil rights period. And I went to Franklin & Marshall, not because I knew anyone. Largely they gave me a great scholarship and I heard they had a strong government department and those were the two things that took me there. And it changed my life."

Going to college in Lancaster turned out to be an excellent decision. "It was the greatest area to grow up in and mature and still be protected, and yet be challenged mentally," she said. "Being pulled away from the urban areas, you don't get the distractions that many others could have had. So I knew I was going to be a political science major, which turned out to be government at F&M. From the very beginning I declared it pretty much as my major."

Dow met Sid Wise shortly after arriving at the College. "I met Sid early on because I had always been active in organizations. I was looking for one and I ended up being on the Student Conduct Committee as a freshman," she says. "Sid Wise was the faculty representative. I got on the Committee as this young kid, and realized that it was a mini, quasi-judiciary type process at the college level. Each year, Sid was right there guiding me through all types of matters, including thefts from the dorms and bigger things. By the end of my college career, he empowered me to run that group, which made some significant decisions on people's lives. That was very much akin to what he did for others, to recognize that you can have these leadership positions. It might seem small back then, but it was big on the campus, and it's no different from where I am right now."

Dow's memory of Sid Wise included the classes he taught. "I remember coming out of his classes and I felt an affinity, which I do even more now, with going back to the founding fathers of this great nation. I'm the new continuing process of the great founding fathers which made America great," Dow explains. "And now that burden and that challenge is on us to take the next step and hand it off to them. I reflect on that now, and it is amazing that I get to be the next one to help mold in some little way, or challenge others to do that, in very much the same sense Sid Wise did that challenge for me. You are a part of the process about the greatness that makes America so different and a successful experiment from other government structures that have tried and floundered in the history of mankind. But we contribute and are making it a success story here in America."

She also recalls the many prominent individuals who would come to the college. "We just had some great government representatives and policymakers come through the department and I went to see every one of them," Dow recalls. "I was always encouraged to do so by Sid Wise. To me, they were cutting edge on what was happening at a very challenging time in our country's history. They were there in Lancaster. I mean it's why my love is with Franklin & Marshall College. It was very much people like Sid Wise that made me be able to say that 30 years later. It's the beauty of that school. If you think about where it is, how unlikely is it that it would turn into such a gem."

Despite her academic success, Dow harbored doubts about her ability to succeed in graduate school. "Even though I did really well academically at F&M, I think I still had doubts about my ability to go at the top level law schools. Sid just told me, go out for it. Apply to

Chicago. Apply to University of Pennsylvania. Ultimately those were the two big schools that I sought out, and I was happy to get accepted ultimately to both of them, and went to Penn."

Dow recalls Wise's desire that students go into public service. "He was always pushing every student in there to go into public service, which definitely is his claim to fame. He'd say, 'What's the problem that we're ultimately trying to address?' whether it's a civil rights issue, a legislative issue, looking at the stories, and that's what was so great about him. He was always going, 'What are the underlying themes and stories that drove this result, and how could it have been changed?' Or, 'How miraculous is it that we got this result given all the factors that surrounded it.' That's what I loved about Franklin & Marshall's Government program. He put you on the spot in class, and I always loved that."

Dow also noted that Professor Wise helped minority students. "In particular, I thought Sid went out of his way to help minorities. That meant a lot to me as an African American going through the college at that time," she recalls. "I have a great respect and admiration for him. Not that he gave you special treatment, but he challenged you and I think sometimes he sensed when you had self-doubt. He pulled you up and told you, 'You can do it and you should look in this direction.' That alone is something I admired and loved in him. He did it in a way that made you feel that he was helping you get there as opposed to following in whatever he told you to do."

Despite her closeness with Professor Wise and the Government Department, Dow notes that ideology was not a factor, which served her well under Chris

Christie. "If anything, the Government Department didn't push their politics; they pushed politics in a purer sense, and the system. The emphasis, for me, was always that the system *is* the people, and you've got to focus on the human element when looking at that. I thought that was really key and helped me interact," she notes.

"Wanting to get in the most challenging environment was in many respects a tribute to him and the school," Dow says, "where they put the confidence into me to know that you could make a difference. As a result I ended up getting in with the southern District of New York. At the time it was making some historic cases in and around the country as it reflected in New York, and ultimately from there I've stayed in government service and prosecution largely ever since."

"My personal experience and life story is in many respects reflective of that. I mean here I am, I am a lifelong Democrat and always will be, and I served as the AG of probably one of the most prominent governors of an opposite party, and we were able to function well and be partners in really challenging economic times. If I had been the polarizing type, there is just no way I would have accepted this challenge or been here at this time. The reality is, it shouldn't be the stark polar opposites, but a blending of the best of what people can contribute."

Overall, Dow recalls her relationship with Professor Wise as the inspiration for her life. "He inspired my great love for that college. Very much stemming from my relationship [with him] and maturation process, an intellectual challenge," she says. "The greatness and the brilliance of Sid Wise is that he wasn't polarizing. What he often focused on was, 'Bring out the best of you and be engaged. Be engaged as part of the process. Don't be so persuaded by the almighty dollar that you've forgotten what made us a nation.'"

# Mary Schapiro – "Think About Government Service"

An anthropology major at F&M, Mary Schapiro graduated in 1977 and received her law degree from George Washington University in 1980. Following law school, she worked as a trial attorney for the Commodity Futures Trading Commission, and then joined the Futures Industry Association as general counsel and senior vice president until her 1988 appointment as Securities and Exchange Commission Commissioner by President Reagan. Schapiro was reappointed by President George H.W. Bush in 1989, then appointed as Chairman of the Federal Commodity Futures Trading Commission by President Clinton in 1994 and as Acting Chairman of SEC in 1994 by President Clinton. In 1996, she joined the National Association of Securities Dealers (NASD) (now the Financial Industry Regulatory Authority) as the president of NASD Regulation. She became the vice chairperson of the NASD in 2002, and in 2006 she became NASD's chairperson and CEO. Appointed by President Obama, Schapiro was sworn in as Chairman of the SEC on January 27, 2009 and was the first woman to serve as the agency's permanent Chairman.

Ms. Schapiro's appointment, during one of the biggest financial crises in U.S. history, was a watershed moment for the SEC. Under her leadership, the SEC brought a record number of enforcement actions and pursued numerous individuals and entities in connection with the financial crisis. Equally important, she strove to restore investor confidence in the market by instituting measures to help reduce the likelihood of another flash crash by restructuring the SEC to become more effective in its investor protection mission.

While at F&M, Ms. Schapiro was influenced dramatically by her introductory course in government, "American Government," and its professor, Sid Wise. "[Sid] just made it so incredibly real and alive – how the government works, how the three branches of government balance each other in power and authority – he just made it so interesting. I will say that it really encouraged me to consider a career in government even as early as freshman year of college and that definitely always stayed with me. I kind of always knew I wanted to go to law school," she notes.

She also was pleased with the government department's focus on people, not theory. "I love the fact that it's called Government and not Political Science and its clear what it is about," she explains. "I certainly didn't have a government family that had any connection to government at all, so it wasn't like it was a burning desire to do public service or anything like that."

As a result of taking that class with Professor Wise, Schapiro developed a strong interest in public service. When I got to law school, I had no interest at all in financial services. One of my lowest grades in law school was in fact securities law, but I wanted to couple my anthropology with law and I thought I would actually try to do something around Native Americans and legal services."

"But when I was getting ready to graduate from law school, I had this – and I really do attribute it to Sid, this call of government and I went to law school in

Washington for lots of exposure to the federal government, but I still had this in the back of my head: *'You should think about government service.'* I had internships when I was in law school in the White House and in the Farm Credit Administration, a network of banks that lent to agricultural businesses and farms. I think I would have been just as happy to be doing public policy in a completely different area, environmental or health or anything. So I went right into a small federal agency that regulated commodity markets at the time."

Schapiro distinctly recalls Professor Wise's style and how he struck chords with his students. "He was just such a profoundly decent intellectual caring person, and if he said to you, 'I think you'd be really good at something,' it was a little bit like, 'If Sid Wise thinks I could do this, I should really think about doing this.'"

"There was this aura about him... he was just one of those people who wouldn't steer you wrong, who really cared deeply about his students, cared deeply about their being successful and going on and becoming something. It was important to him, I think, for people to go into government. My sense was, from my conversations with him, that he took a lot of pride in the fact that people went on to pursue careers in government."

"He didn't get off into Democrats versus Republicans or liberals versus conservatives, it was much more about how government works. This left me with a view that I wholeheartedly subscribe to today, [which] is that government can be an enormous force for good and solve a lot of problems," she explains. "Not every problem, but it can solve a lot of problems and I think that's why people loved that introductory course.

It left you with this view that government is important. Yeah, entrepreneurship is important, and building solid business is important. All those things matter, but we don't often think about government as anything but sort of big and evil and you don't leave that course feeling that way. You leave it feeling that it can be a tremendous positive force in society."

"It's not that we're going to get it right in government every time, but if people have the will in government to do the right thing, to work together, to build the alliances and to build on the compromises, we're going to solve these problems. I'm absolutely convinced we're going to solve these problems. It's kind of painful getting there, we're going to be making up for a lot of sins over the last couple of decades, but we'll get there if people are willing to give it everything they've got."

Like so many other students, she also visited with Professor Wise. "You never felt that you were imposing on his time when you went to see him. You never felt like he'd rather be talking to the smarter person sitting next to you, because there were a lot of smarter people than I was. He never made you feel that because you were a woman you were not the absolute equal and absolutely worthy of every minute you wanted that he would give you," she notes. "As a result, F&M was great foundation for law school, for thinking, for being willing to step outside the comfort zone."

Schapiro even recalls one of her exams with Professor Wise. "There was a set of questions on the judiciary, a set of questions on the executive branch, and a set of questions on the legislative branch. I took the test, and I turned in my three blue books. And he called me into his office the next day, and he said, 'You are such a good student, and you have really done really thoughtful answers to all these questions on the executive branch, and all these questions on the legislative branch. What happened to you on the Supreme Court?' I said, 'I studied too much of the other two and not enough of that one,' and – I've never forgotten it because I was always reminded that the Supreme Court is equally important, except that I didn't treat it that way on the test. I just remember we had a very good long talk about it. Calling me in and really talking through, it was a very human, decent thing to do."

# Robert Friedrich – He Always Had the Right Advice

Associate Professor of Government Robert Friedrich joined the F&M faculty in 1976 and recalls that Sidney was the one who was the most approachable, friendly, and avuncular. He would kind of take you under his wing and give advice. He would sometimes offer advice about various things, and people thought that Sid and Dick and John ran the college."

Moreover, the Government Department "was viewed as being the most powerful department. Sid, Dick and John, but especially Sid, were seen as the sages of the college. Sidney was very astute politically, and if you were trying to get something done, Sidney would have very good advice about how to do it. All three of them were very sharp politically, but Sidney worked more informally in a lot of cases and behind the scenes. That was probably easier to do in those days because back then there was a college senate, which was faculty and students. You could imagine Sidney taking a student aside to talk to them about what might be a good thing to happen in the next senate meeting."

Another difference Friedrich recalls about his transition to academia was that "In graduate school, you never learn anything about how to be a professor. All you learn about is political science, how the government works, public opinion, and stuff like that. In those days there was really no formal instruction in how to teach. The only experience that you would have generally was if you were a teaching assistant for some other professor, but even then you were very much an employee, and you didn't have much autonomy," he recalls.

"Students would come into your office and say start to cry because you had given them a C or something like that, and say, 'This is going to ruin my life. I will never get into law school!' What do I say? 'I don't think it's going to ruin your life, right?' I remember once I was all rattled because in Gov 80 [Political Research], the students were very upset that one of the exams I had given was too long. And so I was telling Sidney that, and he said, 'Bob, I've never had a student complain that an exam was too short.' He certainly believed you should take what students had to say seriously, but that you also needed to keep it in perspective, and that's an important thing for a beginning professor because you tend to be really worried about antagonizing the students. You think, 'Oh if I do something they think is mean, then they're going to give me bad teaching evaluations. Then I won't get tenure,' but he was always very calm and reassuring about those kinds of things, and always leavened it with a sense of humor. I think Sidney left a number of legacies to the department, and that's one of them," he notes. "The other is this notion of preparing students for public service and then doing so much to actually help them get their foot in the door to start to be public servants. I was the chair of the Sidney Wise Public Internship Committee for about five or six years, ending a couple years ago, but Sidney did so much in terms of helping students who then ended up in places where they were able to help other students get internships and jobs. I don't think anybody here is as good at that as Sidney was, but we still think it's important and like to do it. That's a way in which I'd say he individually has really set sort of the pillar of the department in terms of what the department sees as its role in educating students."

Friedrich also recalls how Sid Wise helped him at a crucial moment in his life. "I had sort of a personal crisis and I went to talk to Sidney about it. He was a very sensitive person and – I'm not trying to be cute, but he was a very wise person. He just had very good advice about how to deal, not just with professional things but also with personal things. I think the other things that always struck me about him – I think lots of people saw him as just this hardcore Democrat. But it was odd because in some ways he was very conservative in his belief in the values of institutions and organization, which were not very popular in the 60s and 70s, [and] were such valuable social assets and infrastructure.

He loved the college for what it sought to do as an institution and for the people who were here. He loved Harvard for basically the same reason. And then he loved the Congress and the Senate. These institutions that some people, especially now, would say, 'Oh they're so dysfunctional, we should get rid of them,' but he saw great value and really great hope in the way institutions like that could work to come to common agreements and achieve things together. He did not like it when people tried to tear down or criticize institutions unfairly. Sidney was not cynical about people or about political and social institutions. He saw them in a very positive way that made people's lives better."

# David Stameshkin – You Need to Talk to Sidney First

David Stameshkin retired in 2012 after a 35-year career at F&M, during which he filled a wide range of positions, including Associate Dean, Prefect of the Bonchek College House (a residence hall), and advisor to the Hillel House (for Jewish students). A beloved fixture at the College, Stameshkin arrived in 1978, facing an uncertain future.

"In 1978, I was hired by the Central Pennsylvania Consortium – Franklin & Marshall, Dickinson, Gettysburg and Wilson – to lead something called The Harrisburg Urban Semester (THUS). Because of that, I had to recruit students from 15 liberal arts colleges in Central Pennsylvania; part of the THUS experience was to write a very lengthy paper integrating theory and practice, and every college allowed me to grade those papers, except for F&M, because they didn't trust this program at all," Stameshkin recalls.

"When I was first hired, Keith Spalding was President. I was in his office, he was the Chair of the Board of the Central Pennsylvania Consortium. He said, 'David, next door is Goethean Hall, there are three men in Goethean Hall that you must get on your side otherwise, you will fail, and you'll be out of here so fast, I won't remember your name, which is hard enough as it is. There's Sidney Wise, John Vanderzell and Dick Schier, go find them, do the right thing; otherwise, bye-bye," says Stameshkin. "That's what he told me; that's the only advice he gave me. So I quickly went over to Goethean, and I guess the directors of this program had been quite a weird lot before me. So I walked in in my three-piece suit, and I said to Sidney, 'Hi, my name is David Stameshkin, I'm the new head of the Harrisburg Urban Semester.' He replied, 'No, you can't be.' 'Why not?' I ask. 'You're wearing a suit, you look half decent. Do you know anything? Sit down. So of course, I'm fairly rattled at this point. But we had a great discussion, and he said he would be glad to help me any way he could. He said, 'Go find my other two guys. Keith Spalding already told me,' he laughed. 'Yes, well, that's Keith, ha, ha.'"

Over the next six years, Stameshkin led the Program and "went to Sidney a lot, because a lot of students in my program worked for the state legislature. My students did an internship, 25 hours a week, and a lot of them wanted to work in the state legislature. Well, he'd written the book on it. But Sidney, because he liked Harrisburg and understood it, was my star, he was very helpful."

"When I came here as a Dean in 1984, he was the first person I went to, and I said, 'What have I gotten myself into?' He laughed, and explained the terrain to me, as he did to so many people. So I've always been in his debt."

Stameshkin also worked closely with Sid Wise when he served as Associate Vice President of Development; Professor Wise joined the Department in 1989. "He came over to the office once a week, and he would start making phone calls to his former students, and the calls were magnificent," notes Stameshkin. "He would say, 'Hello, Bill, this is Sidney Wise – and there'd be this pause because they'd say something. Sometimes it was like, I turned that paper in, I know I turned that paper in.' This is like the Class of '61 or something. They

175

would then say, 'you know, I know I did, you know. And they were just hysterical. He'd come and tell me at the end of the day, 'Well, David, I had some really good ones today. And they gave donations to the College too.' You couldn't say no to him."

Stameshkin notes that Wise worked with all students, although a disproportionate number of African-American and Jewish students benefited from his efforts. "If you were a Jewish or African-American student, and you saw a Jewish faculty member – there weren't very many where it made difference. One-half of one percent of Lancaster County is Jewish. So these kids are here, they're used to being from fairly Jewish places, like suburban Philadelphia and suburban New York, and they come here, they're told, 'You walk outside the college community, there's nothing, this is it,' so you look for people to whom you can relate. He could deal with a lot of different kinds of people, you could feel very comfortable with that; he could take African-Americans because he really wanted to do something, it was a justice thing for him."

Another side of Wise that was rarely seen was his religious side. "Sid used to be active in our Synagogue, where he taught confirmation classes," notes Stameshkin. Although Wise rarely discussed religion, he and Stameshkin "would shut the door and we'd talk, because [Stameshkin] was the first Jewish administrator at F&M except for Ken Duberstein.'"

Finally, Stameshkin recalls receiving "interior political advice" from Wise. "When I became Assistant to President Kneedler, I went over and talked to [Sidney], and he gave me some really good advice about how to deal with faculty in that position. He was my guide. Dick Kneedler used to send me to him sometimes. Dick would say, 'I don't know how the faculty would take something. Would you mind going and talking to Sidney a little bit?' So I'd go talk to Sidney. "

# James Spencer – He Always Listened and Saw Your Point of View

Although Sid Wise and Chemistry Professor Jim Spencer "were on different poles politically, but we always found common ground and [Spencer] always found him to be extraordinarily fair." It was the events that occurred when Professor Spencer arrived on campus in 1980 that helped foster and cement their relationship.

"When I first came, one of the first official college get-togethers was about the time that Sid and I began to have lunches and conversations. At that time, Jeanne Kirkpatrick was the U.S. Representative to the United Nations and she was being asked to come to F&M to be the Commencement speaker. There was immediate reaction to it, as you might imagine, from faculty. There was a meeting of the faculty in order to express views about this because there were many faculty who thought that we should not ask her, principally I think, because she was Republican. One of the things that I remember at the first meeting was when Sid stood up in front of the faculty and said, "Here are the problems. You're talking about a vote that was taken at the World Health Organization, not at the United Nations. Jeanne Kirkpatrick did not vote on this. The vote had something to do with distributing food [Nestle infant formula] to children in Africa, I think, or something like that, or something about milk, or something like that. He went through the list and ticked them off the things that were brought up against her and should disallow her from talking here. This was, of course, Sid, who was very much a Democrat, standing up for someone who was very much a Republican. I felt at that point we had a lot in common."

"Sid was always fair and approachable and listening, and able to see your point of view and to consider that, well, maybe I'm right and maybe I'm wrong in this, let's talk about this. He was, even though I knew him only as a friend, influential in the way that he conducted himself, which was the way I thought faculty members should conduct themselves."

"He was [also] very caring in that he was involved very closely with a lot of people in Washington. He was able to arrange for internships and do the kinds of things that he thought would benefit his students. He was absolutely balanced. Even though it was clear which side he generally would come down on, he never said, 'You can't think that way,' or, 'You've got to be an idiot to think like that.' He always respected other people's opinions and that to me was a very important part of knowing Sid for the time that I did."

"When Sid died, the College lost one of the pillars of one of our strongest departments. We lost a lot of influence in Washington and locally with politics. He was known by almost everybody. He was a mentor to so many people who had gone on and gave him additional options for those people who were coming up. It was a real loss to the college. Those kinds of people come along once in a very long while. Sid was, I think, unique in many ways and he contributed a lot more to the college than the college ever contributed to him, and that's the way you ought to be, I think, in any organization. There's such an incredible chain of prominent people in Washington who came from this tiny little school. It was remarkable how well known

179

and how respected he was. But you look at the achievements of most of those people who went on, [they were] pretty substantial. He was that middle-of-the-road guy who could see both sides of the road and he knew where he wanted to get to, and he knew how to get people to places where the road forked to go."

"I remember his saying that the most important thing for him when he was retired was that he be within walking distance of a deli and he could get the *New York Times* every day. He said, 'Nothing else matters.'"

# Lawrence Stengel – Sid Wise is the Reason I Am a Judge

Lawrence Stengel's resume is typical of many judges. Stengel, a Lancaster native who sits on the U.S. District Court for the Eastern District of Pennsylvania, was a practicing attorney who had aspired to become a judge. Fortunately, there was an opening on the local trial court, and the alumnus of St. Joseph's University and the University of Pittsburgh School of Law applied. But as he recalls, "Sid Wise is a major reason why I am a judge. I didn't know him. I had no connection with him, but I learned long after the fact how that had played out, so I think I owe my getting that appointment to his advocacy and I never knew it."

"I was practicing law in Lancaster in 1990, and there was an opening on the Court of Common Pleas of Lancaster County, because Judge Ronald Buckwalter was appointed by the first President Bush to come down to this court to become a judge of the Eastern District," Stengel explains. "Governor Casey appointed a five person nominating committee to receive applications and interview interested people, and then make recommendations to the governor. "

"So I interviewed with the committee. I was 37 years old and really didn't think it was going to go my way. I figured I would just get my name out there," Stengel recalls. "On the committee was Sid Wise, of the Franklin & Marshall Government Department. There were a lot of people who interviewed and I remember the interview being very interesting and Sid Wise was a very active questioner. I didn't know him personally. I knew him by reputation. My brother had been an

American studies major at Franklin & Marshall and knew of Sid and my mother was one of the nurses in the infirmary so we knew a lot of people at F&M. And so I knew of Sid by his wonderful reputation."

"What I learned in the process was – and this is hearsay from other people who were on the committee – that the governor wanted a list of – I've heard three, I've heard five names – but I heard that Sid Wise insisted that they prioritize the names and he wanted me at the top of the list and he wanted to personally deliver the list to the governor. So he and someone else from the committee drove up to Harrisburg to deliver the list. I don't know if it was delivered to the governor or it was to the governor's council, but he wanted to communicate in person who they wanted to fill the position."

What is perhaps most interesting is that Stengel was appointed to fill Judge Buckwalter's seat on the Lancaster court. Then, when Judge Buckwalter took senior status, Stengel was nominated and approved to fill Judge Buckwalter's seat on the federal bench.

Since becoming a judge, Stengel has greatly expanded his connection with F&M. He teaches a course every spring. He has now developed a much stronger connection, teaching a course "Trial Courts and the Justice System," every spring. In addition, "When law clerk applications come in, I always search for F&M people. I've had people in the college contact me about certain people and I've hired them. I've had professors in the government department and people in the administration contact me and I feel that, because of my relationship with the college, they feel comfortable doing that." In sum, Judge Stengel has become another page in the Sid Wise Rolodex.

# Douglas Arpert – All of the Apprehension & Anxiety Disappeared

Currently a Magistrate Judge for the United States District Court for the District of New Jersey, Douglas Arpert graduated from F&M in 1981 and received his law degree from Emory University. Part of the inspiration for his career came during his first semester at F&M, when the "very first class [he] went to was Government 11 [American Government] with Professor Wise – first semester, first year, first class. He was short, stocky, but very energetic, a determined looking guy. In he walks, and he plops his folder down, hops up on the desk and sits with his legs dangling over the front of the desk, sitting on his hands leaning forward. And he just started talking. Suddenly all of that apprehension and all of that anxiety about whether I was going to be okay in that environment began to evaporate. And I realized this guy is human and he's very user friendly, and he was my first exposure."

Of course, having the most senior faculty in the Government Department teach the introductory course is often cited as the key reason so many students eventually decided to major in government at the College. "I think it's a brilliant approach," says Arpert, "because you can imagine another philosophy, which is you put your rookies on the task of teaching the intro courses. When Sid Wise taught Gov 11, he had a disarming way of making everybody feel comfortable – but then he launched into the subject matter, and delivered it in a way that was just so interesting. He hooked a lot of us."

Wise also remained an ambassador for the College. During the 1980s, the College de-recognized all of the fraternities, upsetting many students and alumni, including Arpert. "I became somewhat disenchanted and disenfranchised myself at some point over the whole fraternity de-recognition issue. At the time, I think I was on the alumni advisory board, I was doing the volunteer admissions interviews for kids. We were very, at that point, connected back to the school. Then the president came along and sort of unilaterally whacked the fraternities. I was upset. I was offended. I expressed that. The response to that, and I'm sure this was just my perspective, was we got cut off. The next thing you know, I was not reappointed to whatever advisory board I was on. I was no longer getting referrals for the admissions interviews. I thought if that's the way you're dealing with dissent in the ranks, then I'm out.

"At some point, not too long after that, don't you know, I get a call from Sid Wise, saying, sort of, 'Where'd you go? What happened? You dropped off the radar screen.' He talked me off the ledge. He didn't undercut the administration, but he said, 'You know it's a change and change is difficult and we need to work through it together and sort of politicked his way through the conversation.' But I was impressed that he took the initiative to reach out to me when I had become sort of cranky about the issue."

# Richard Plepler – "I looked up to Sid as the standard of wisdom, judgment, insight."

According to the *New York Times*, Richard Plepler, the chief executive of HBO, occupies a role that goes well beyond television and extends into New York's political, media and entertainment cliques: "For a decade, Mr. Plepler has hosted dinner parties at his five-story town house on the Upper East Side with his wife, Lisa, where a parade of guests, including Israel's president, Shimon Peres; the scholar Henry Louis Gates Jr.; and the NBC News anchor Brian Williams, discuss foreign policy and domestic affairs. Political candidates seek his counsel. And since 2007, when Mr. Plepler began overseeing programming at HBO, he has used his influence to produce shows based on political events."[7] Plepler's focus on political events arose from his relationship with his college professor, Sid Wise, with whom he never took a course.

"I didn't even have him as a formal professor," Plepler explains, "but in many respects that's even more interesting, because while I didn't have him, I looked up to Sid as the standard of wisdom, judgment, insight. To me, he was the personification not only of what a great educator would be, but he was the personification of what a great citizen should be; engaged, committed, teaching, contributing, lending wisdom, sharing wisdom. I would always go talk to him about politics and world affairs."

---

[7] http://www.nytimes.com/2012/09/23/fashion/richard-plepler-of-hbo-stands-tall-in-new-yorks-cultural-elite.html?pagewanted=all

This insight helped Plepler focus his career. "I was always touched by his engagement with my passion. I always knew this is a guy who looked at my love of public policy and political discourse, and he shared himself with me. And I imputed to him all that was best about the school, civic engagement, and the requirements of citizenry. I looked at him and I said, 'This is how you behave as a citizen. You have no other choice but that level of engagement,' and he really set a standard for me."

After graduating from F&M, Plepler served as an aide to Senator Christopher Dodd of Connecticut; he then founded and headed a communications consulting and production firm, RLP Inc., and produced several TV documentaries for Public Television. He remains particularly proud of a film he produced before joining HBO, which caught the attention of Professor Wise.

"In 1987 or '88, before I came here [to HBO], I made a documentary on the First Intifada. I was in my little office, and I got a call from my old professor, eight years out of school. He said, 'I watched your film and I was so taken by what you had done and that you wrote it. I am so proud of you, and I wondered if you might come back to school and speak to the kids.' I said, 'I'd be thrilled to,' and I came back. I was probably 29. We showed the film, and then I did a talk and a Q&A after the film."

Professor Wise's praise struck a deep chord with Plepler. "His praise to me was so meaningful, I remember kind of saying to myself, '"Well if Sid Wise tells me that I really not only can frame the world this way, but present it this way, maybe that's really something that he felt."' Plepler recalls returning to

F&M in the mid-90s to give a talk, and attending a dinner at home of the President of College. "I just got up very spontaneously to give a toast to all of them, because I thought they were all so extraordinary. And I said, 'I don't know how many times people have the privilege of being able to come back here and say thank you, but I've now been out maybe a dozen years. I've met a lot of people, I've seen a lot. I have never encountered a collection of people who are smarter, wiser, more interesting to engage with and talk to, and finer human beings and citizens than the group of people who I studied with from 1977 to 1981. I just want to thank you all.' Sid Wise was the epitome of what I meant by that toast. To this day, where I've been so fortunate to encounter so many people in government and politics and business at the highest levels, I look back at the training and encounters that I had with all of them, Sid being the granddaddy of that group, and I just said, 'They set me on my way.' I don't think that that there is a higher compliment that a student can pay to his teacher than 28 years later or something, feeling the same level of gratitude, respect and appreciation for the anchoring that they gave.

Plepler recalls Wise's connection with him and other students. "I think that he possessed a quality – I'm really relating an emotional connection, which at the same time is pedagogical, but he possessed that gift. I think because he was the highest standard, he showed you that highest standard, and showed you that film, culture, journalism, literature, music and cigars were part of living a fully engaged life. That the compendium of these things, the way in which all these things interrelated; film was as important to understanding culture as politics or journalism was, which was as important as studying the body politic, which was as important as understanding the music of it. So he was a complete educator in the broadest sense of the word. The fact that I think of him, Stan [Michalak], Bob [Gray] and Joe [Karlesky], all with that level of reverence and respect is really the greatest legacy that you can leave, having that kind of memory. I mean, short of family, it's hard to think of a connection that could compete with that."

"I think if you define what an educator in the pure sense would hope to do, it would be to give you both the tools and the framework and the confidence to see, in Norman Lear's phrase, your ability to fill your own silhouette. And I think that Sid showed you that there was a big silhouette to fill, and you should fill it. So I think that it's probably the case that whether you're speaking to Stan [Michalak] or whether you're speaking to Duberstein or whether you're speaking to any of the people who've gone on to do so well, they saw their potential through Sid, and that was one of his great gifts."

"That's why I invoked the film. I mean, that was one of his passions. That's why I raised the interaction between culture politics and his film series. I saw those things for the first time with Sid Wise, and they had a huge impact. And of course, my migration to this business was no surprise, and my passion for films on world affairs and politics and Churchill and African-American history are inspired by that chain of passions that he carried with him."

"Sid understood you have to share in the actions and passions of your time, and I think what he was saying all the time is that however you do it, share in the actions and passions, and participate, engage, be a part of it," Plepler recalls. "He touched so many people who've gone on to have an impact. I always remember his words to me, 'No matter how comfortable or competent you are, hearing from somebody you really respect that you have 'the goods,' has tremendous meaning.'"

"He was the real deal, he was an original, and he had impact in the best way. If you have to go and cultivate power, you don't have it. If it flows to you, you have it. And he had real power because you wanted to be in his orbit. You wanted to hear what he had to say. You wanted his judgment. That's real authority, and that's real wisdom. He was the personification of a teacher. He was the personification of the standard."

"He was a remarkable guy, and he had the gift of connecting. And I think he had the gift of connecting because he saw in you that part of you that was the best of yourself, and he encouraged it. Having the impact that he had is a gift from God. It's really the story of the power of a great mentor, power of a great educator, with a lot of different, interesting people just talking about him."

# Daniel J. Siegel – "I always knew you could do it. You had to learn it for yourself"

Dear Dan:

I was so pleased to hear of your becoming a partner. Surely it must be one of life's great moments, somewhat more significant than becoming an editor & less significant than becoming a father. Congratulations & best wishes – you earned it & deserved it. You realize of course that your wife deserves the lion's share of the credit.

Stay well,

Sid Wise      7/25 [1992]

\*\*\*\*\*\*

As a freshman at Franklin and Marshall College in 1977, I had much of the baggage every student probably carries. Confident in my abilities, I questioned other skills, especially the ability to work with and lead others. When I arrived at F&M, my schedule included one science course, either chemistry or biology; I knew that if I took the course –filled with pre-meds – I would not be happy, and neither would my grade. So I went to meet with my designated advisor, Government Professor Sidney Wise. I had no idea who he was.

I remember entering Professor Wise's office, a small smoke-filled room with floor to ceiling bookcases. He met with me, asked why I was there, and I explained why I needed to take a different class. He looked at me with some disdain, and inquired why I was so certain that I did not belong in that class. I do not remember my answer, but was thrilled and relieved when he approved my switching to a course known as "Baby Physics."

For whatever reason, still unclear after all these years, Professor Wise took me under his wing and suggested that I join *The College Reporter*, the college's weekly newspaper. During my freshman year, much happened on campus. I quickly rose through the ranks of *The College Reporter* and was appointed News Editor. In addition, my assignments included covering the filming and world premiere of *The Boys From Brazil*, a movie directed by F&M alumnus Franklin J. Schaffner. During every Schaffner-related event, be it a news conference, the granting of honorary degrees to Schaffner and film stars Gregory Peck and Laurence Olivier, or the film's world premiere on campus, I was there reporting the events, with Sid almost always at my side.

By the conclusion of my sophomore year, I had become *The College Reporter*'s Managing Editor, and everyone expected me to become editor at the end of my junior year. That was not to be, and therein lies the genesis of Sid's note card.

Rather than following the tradition in which the outgoing editor selected the incoming one, the College surprisingly decreed that the staff would elect the incoming editor. Things did not go well. While the staff respected my writing skills, some questioned my leadership skills, and I was not elected Editor. I was distraught, and sought the solace of Dr. Wise. He consoled me, explaining that what happened was wrong and had nothing to do with me, my skills or leadership abilities. As a 20-year-old, I could not see beyond the rejection, and vowed never to seek an editorship – of anything – ever.

Dr. Wise then made a suggestion that changed my life, although I did not know it then. He suggested that I apply for a job as a stringer, *i.e.*, a part-time free-lance reporter, for the *Lancaster Intelligencer-Journal*, the local morning newspaper. I was hired, wrote sports and features, and loved the job.

My work on the *Intell* (as it was known) turned out to be invaluable. There, I learned to write well, quickly, succinctly, and on deadline, skills that have proven invaluable as a lawyer. It is safe to say that not becoming editor was the **best** thing that happened to me professionally. I also matured and learned skills I could never have acquired at *The College Reporter*. These talents have been essential to my career, which focuses on writing briefs and other documents not only for my clients, but also for other lawyers and their clients.

I graduated from F&M in 1981 with honors in government; Sid was one of my advisors for the honors thesis comparing the newspaper coverage by the Lancaster daily newspapers of the 1980 Presidential election. We stayed in touch, and he took a keen interest in my personal and professional lives. He answered calls, responded to letters, and was always there for me.

In addition, I took to heart Sid's perspective on government – that you accomplish more, and are more effective, by being cordial, by listening, by being willing

193

to compromise, by not being negative, by not being hostile, and never burning bridges. Still, at times I questioned my leadership ability.

In 1989, I was elected President of the Associated Stamp Clubs of Southeastern Pennsylvania and Delaware. My election was controversial, as were some of the actions taken by the Board under my leadership. First, I eliminated those who created most of the controversy. Second, I changed the organization's name to the Philadelphia National Stamp Exhibition, arguing that the name needed to reflect who we were to non-collectors. Finally, I hired a public relations company, something no other national show had ever done.

The results were tangible. Attendance increased dramatically, dealer sales improved, and one leading philatelic commentator honored our "imagineering." I was hailed as a leader, the trait I had doubted because of *The College Reporter*. I called Sid to tell him of my success. His reply: "I always knew you could do it. You had to learn it for yourself."

As always, Sid's message could not have been clearer: I needed to recognize my strengths and weaknesses, and work hard to improve the weaknesses so that they could become additional strengths. In addition, I should not worry what everyone else says because at times life is not fair and critics are wrong. Instead, I needed to have confidence in myself and my leadership abilities. Learning this lesson took a long time, and I continue to learn it.

In 1992, I became a partner in my law firm. Again, Sid was there, this time with his note card, which reminds me of what matters most: my wife, Eileen (the same name as Sid's wife), and now my two sons, Bradley and Douglas (Douglas was born in 1994, the year Sid died, and his middle name, Steven, was chosen in Sid's honor).

In 2005, I opened my own law firm and a technology consulting firm for lawyers. I was scared. My confidence would wax and wane, and every time it did I remembered Sid's words.

There is more to the story. I was elected a Commissioner in Haverford Township in a 2008 special election, and re-elected for a full term in 2009. For those who voted against me to become Editor, my election must have been a surprise. But because I try to utilize the skills Sid emphasized – especially civility and compromise – I am proud to be viewed as reasonable and as someone whose voice is sought.

To bring things full circle, in July 2011 I became the Editor of *The Philadelphia Lawyer,* the quarterly magazine published by the Philadelphia Bar Association. I was no longer afraid of becoming an Editor, and I'm sure Sid is smiling down at me right now.

# Nanine Hartzenbusch – "Take Every Student Seriously"

When people think of government/political science students, they assume they will become lawyers, business people and politicians, not photographers. But a picture can be worth a thousand words, and some of history's greatest events are remembered more by a photo than any other characteristic. For Nanine Hartzenbusch, her passion was photography, yet she also wanted to study government, and she turned to Sid Wise for guidance. In 1992, she was part of a team of photojournalists awarded the Pulitzer Prize for coverage of the Union Square Subway crash in New York.

Hartzenbusch worked for *New York Newsday*, the Associated Press, and the *Baltimore Sun*; she has also covered a wide range of events, including Presidential and Papal visits, political protests, and parades. Her first support came while in college where, although she aspired to a government career, her love of photography was even greater. "My dad was a newsman with the *Associated Press*, so I was born into a journalism family, and I was not expected to follow in his footsteps because I wanted to be a foreign service officer and work as a diplomat," she remembers. "So I took international relations classes at F&M, and majored in government, but I always had my camera with me and I always was taking pictures, and I found myself going in that direction, running the college darkroom, teaching classes."

She recalls that Sid Wise "was just a real support to my desire to become a photojournalist, or to work for newspapers. While at F&M, I worked for *The Washington Star* newspaper during one January break when we had six weeks off, and I would always come back to Sid and tell him about my experiences. In addition, he and I corresponded for quite a few years after graduation, and he was always encouraging me in that direction when F&M wasn't known for photojournalism or for newspapers."

Like other alumni, Hartzenbusch did not take that many classes with Sid Wise. She took his "film class, and loved that, of course; but he was more of a confidante, and more of a person to whom I would report my experiences. He would encourage me, give me advice about careers and that sort of thing, where nobody else at the school really was qualified, or felt they were qualified, or were able to help me because they were involved in other areas," she explains.

"I really trusted him, and he was so positive and encouraging about my career goals, even when I think 90 percent of the people we went to school with became doctors, lawyers, or were MBAs. But I don't know of anyone else who went to work for a newspaper or wanted to work for a newspaper," she explains. "I always felt that the liberal arts education was the best preparation for any kind of career in a newspaper. I felt sort of smug and a little bit superior to my colleagues at the newspapers who majored in journalism or majored in photojournalism, because I felt that that was more of a craft that they had learned at school, but they weren't exploring all these other topics. A liberal arts education teaches you a little bit about a lot, and teaches you to be curious and to look up information, those interview skills, and all that stuff that really helped me in my career. As a visual journalist, the craft and the technical

197

stuff are very important, but you can learn that skill. I think the other part is even more important, developing story ideas, researching topics, and coming up with proposals to do stories – those are the really important stories that you can do at a newspaper, alongside with reacting to fires and murders, and that sort of thing."

Hartzenbusch recalls that Professor Wise "really encouraged people to explore different careers. I think he was really excited when I came back from working in Washington, and then the following year, I worked at *The Arkansas Gazette* in Little Rock, which was a totally different experience. In 1981, *The Washington Star* folded. I worked there as an intern in the winter term, and then they asked me to return in the summer; and during that summer, in August, the paper closed. The managing editor of *The Washington Star* went on to be the editor of *The Arkansas Gazette*, and I sent him a letter asking if I could work there during those six weeks. [Sid] truly understood what that experience would bring me and how that would shape me for my future, what doors would open, and how I could parlay that into a job, because you know, with journalism, yes, your education is important and they do want you to have a four-year degree, but really, experience is as important or more important, and they're going to look at that experience that you've had so that you can get your first job. So he was very encouraging."

In retrospect, she treasures the experience at F&M. "We had it really good there. We had a great experience having that connection with our professors; I would have never had something like my friendship with Sid Wise had I gone to a larger school. He brings back such warm feelings about F&M; I have to say, probably if it weren't for him, I may have transferred out. I think he really was the glue that held me there, there were so many reasons why I stayed at F&M and why I enjoyed F&M, but he was certainly a big part of it.

"When I worked for newspapers, I always had ideas about things I wanted to do that were beyond my daily assignments, but it was sometimes hard to find an ear, or someone who has the power to get things published in the newspaper who will listen to you. I feel like Sid was that person for me in college before I even knew that I needed to find that person. So I think that Sid was that person for me at F&M, that he wasn't necessarily the person I took a lot of classes with or anything, but he was very interested in media in general, and knew things about it, studied it and understood it. If I told him things about my experience in the newsroom, he would get it, and he would understand what I had experienced, or he would know the path that I needed to take. He understood the visual medium, and a lot you can transfer – light, in terms of lighting and mood and emotion to photography; film is a whole different genre, but there are many, many similarities. And I felt that when I was speaking to him or talking to him about things, he understood it because he had a visual appreciation."

# Barry Kasinitz – "The people on the other side of an issue, the people of the other party, (a) are certainly not evil, and (b) they actually have something worthwhile to say"

When Barry Kasinitz, the Director of Governmental Affairs for the International Association of Firefighters addressed his organization's 2012 Legislative Conference, he followed Congressman Steve LaTourette and commented that the Congressman's speech demonstrated that "the boss learned more from the intern than the intern learned from the boss." As noted by Ken Duberstein and others, when former students would contact Sid Wise for advice, he would often note that he had become the student and the student was now the teacher.

For Kasinitz, the transition from student to teacher came over time. Yet because of his strong political views, his relationship with Sid Wise differed from others'. "I came to college already bitten with the bug [of politics]. I was working on campaigns as a teenager," says Kasinitz. "I put together a high school political organization. Originally, it was a Democratic organization and then I veered off and I made it an independent group and we interviewed Democratic and Republican candidates. Eventually the Democratic Party in my town asked me to become a committeeman. So when I came to Lancaster, I immediately got involved in Lancaster Democratic politics, and was elected the treasurer of the Democratic committee in the city, and also the leader in ward 9, the college ward."

Kasinitz' selection of F&M was merely happenstance. "I graduated high school early and instead of going to college I was working for the Westchester New York County Executive. I was also able to get a job working for the Speaker of the House in the New York State Assembly, which was phenomenal. So I was going to go to University of Albany and taking classes, but what I was really going to do was to work in the Speaker's office. The Speaker got defeated in the primary and I lost my job and needed to find a college. Well there was this school I didn't even know anything about, but my guidance counselor really liked it. I applied mostly to make him happy. Okay, 'I'll go to F&M,' I told him."

Kasinitz eventually selected government as his major and "When [he] had to pick an advisor, Sid was the guy. There was just something about him. So approachable. He was somebody I wanted to help guide me because he was just that kind of personality. I took a couple of courses with him and then most importantly, did an independent study with him on the legislative operation in the House."

"He got me involved in The Harrisburg Urban Semester. I took a semester in Harrisburg. This was originally his suggestion, and he plugged me into some amazing people. That semester was probably the best experience of my college years." Like many government majors, Kasinitz thought about attending law school. "I did not want to go to law school, and he and I debated that a lot. He really wanted me to. But I remember graduation day and my parents came and I happened to see Sid on the street and introduced them. I remember the very first thing he said to them; he said, *'Your son is just so busy.'* And what he meant was, I didn't want to

201

take a long-term view. And he was absolutely right. I wanted to jump. I wanted to go here. I wanted to go there. And for me it was the Harrisburg semester linked into campaign work which linked into lobbying, and he was always so good about helping – he never would criticize me. He let me know he disagreed, but he was always so good at forcing me to look at the longer term. So it was a fun debate we used to have."

Sid's influence continued well after Kasinitz graduated from F&M and became the chief lobbyist for firefighters in Washington. "I stayed in touch with Sid after school and if anything, we even talked more then. Now, everyone's an expert on everything. But in the days before CNN and cable television, Sid still had such a great sense of things. And it always amazed me, so I kept in touch with him."

In particular, as a lobbyist, Kasinitz appreciated Wise's perspective that all views matter. "Definitely the most important [perspective I gained] by far was the whole idea that the people on the other side of an issue, the people of the other party, (a) are certainly not evil, and (b) they actually have something worthwhile to say. It's not black and white. Sid, constantly was engaging people, and said, *'Never tell anybody they're wrong.'* He would debate you and he would show respect for every point of view. And that has just been so extremely valuable to me that – I give my friends on the Hill a hard time [who don't always embrace that view]."

"I'm pretty hard core Democrat personally on every issue down the line," Kasinitz notes, but that has not limited his relationship on Capitol Hill. "You'll find me taking the liberal standpoint. Yet most of my friends on the Hill are actually Republicans. And that's not something I could have gotten without his perspective; he really taught me to appreciate other people's point of view and listen. In fact, when Sid revised one of the Pennsylvania politics books, he actually cited some of my research on that."

Kasinitz still recalls Professor Wise's advice. "He was always trying to get me looking longer term. There's such great opportunity, I have to jump on it. And [he would say] *'Look, if you're good, there are always going to be opportunities.'* That's a piece of advice I have shared many times with interns I've had over the years. You don't have to do everything today. You don't have to jump all the time and that piece of advice has certainly stuck with me."

# Kenneth Mehlman – "Civility In Politics Is Critical"

Ken Mehlman has long been associated with the Republican Party. He was Chief of Staff for Congresswoman Kay Granger, and on the staff of Congressman Lamar Smith. He has also worked on numerous election campaigns, including the Presidential campaigns of George H.W. Bush (1992), Bob Dole (1996) and George W. Bush (2000). Mehlman then served as George W. Bush's White House Political Director from 2001 to 2004, was campaign manager for Bush-Cheney in 2004, and was Chair of the Republican National Committee from 2005 to 2007. Mehlman is currently a member and Head of Global Public Affairs for Kohlberg Kravis Roberts & Co. Throughout his career, his connections with Professor Wise and the F&M Government Department helped define his career.

Like many other students, Mehlman never took a course with Sid Wise. However, that did not prevent him from seeking Wise's guidance during a key moment in his life. "In 1988 I had just gotten into a number of different law schools and ended up going to Harvard. At the time, it was also the '88 presidential campaign, and I liked George Bush," he explains.

"I remember going to see Sid and getting his advice about being involved in the campaign. It was the week after Bush had come in third in the Iowa caucuses. We talked about whether it made sense for me to get involved in the campaign or go to law school. And he said, 'go to law school.' He was a guy that was worth talking to and had good advice and was generous in his spirit; and so in all ways was an important guy to have conversations with."

Mehlman also acquired his desire to be a more centrist Republican from his relationship with the Government Department. "The most important thing that we can do," he notes, "is to give people practical tools they can use to achieve success and figure out what they want to do with their lives, and have happy, productive, fulfilled lives. I think a big part of that is the liberal arts background, but a big part of it also is skills – *real* skills that can be used."

He also agreed with Sid Wise's belief that civility in politics is critical. "I think that the civil approach is something that I think I get from who I am, my family, my parents – that's just how I was raised – that's the right way to be – incivility is stupid. I remember I was once on one of those point/counterpoint television shows. The other guest said I hate Democrats and all they stand for, and he hated Republicans and all they stand for. He asked me if I hated Democrats and I said, 'My whole family is Democrats and there are a lot of reasons to hate them apart from their politics. And we laughed – but I just find that to be inconceivable, and just crazy. So I think that that is very much consistent with the approach Sid took."

Another reason why Mehlman benefited from his F&M education was "the fact that F&M was a government department, not political science. Simply providing a place where people can think and learn and make friends is nice, but it's not going to cause them to spend $40,000 to $50,000 a year in tuition, in every case.

I think that bringing in the political center is a huge step in that direction," and that was part of the legacy he acquired from Sid Wise.

# Jonathan Blyth – "The Keeper of the Capital Hill Scorecard"

When you visit Jonathan Blyth's condominium, you are immediately struck by the view – his balcony looks directly at the Iwo Jima Memorial, with the Washington Monument, Lincoln Memorial, and the Capitol directly in view; Arlington National Cemetery is to your right. The view is quintessential Washington. And that is why Jonathan Blyth lives there.

"I tell this story, that when I first came to Washington, I used to go to Arlington Cemetery and come to the Iwo Jima Memorial and I used to look up at this building and I said, 'If I ever make it in Washington, this is where I want to live, and waking up and looking at that view, which I think is one of the most beautiful views in the United States of the Capitol and the Washington Monument and the Lincoln Memorial is really what Sid Wise taught us to love about Washington," Blyth reminisces.

Blyth is currently Chief of Staff to Florida Congressman Allen West, but his biography drips of Washington and public service. Blyth has worked for more than 20 years in the Legislative and Executive Branches of the federal government. He has served on the Congressional staffs of several members of Congress in both the House of Representatives and the United States Senate, including serving as the Chief of Staff for Congressman Bob Barr (R-GA) and Congressman Bill Martini (R-NJ). Blyth was also a presidential appointee for President George W. Bush in two federal agencies. A graduate of Franklin & Marshall College with a degree in Government, he has a Master's Degree in Public

Administration from George Washington University and a Master's Degree in National Security and Strategic Studies from the Naval War College. He is also a Lieutenant Commander in the United States Navy Reserve. In short, he is a classic Washington insider. Yet his roots and his culture come from his connections with Sid Wise.

Blyth selected F&M because "it was the quintessential experience that [he] wanted in a college." Even so, he got more than he expected. "When I got to Franklin Marshall, it was probably the most difficult academic experience I ever, ever had. When I went to graduate school after Franklin Marshall, I graduated GW with a 3.9 average because I would write papers that these professors had never envisioned. My colleagues, my fellow students, could not write 30-page papers with 150 footnotes. I could, and that was because of Franklin and Marshall," Blyth recalls.

Although he only took one course with Sid Wise, the Government Department quickly made an impact on Blyth. "My first government class was with Professor Vanderzell, and my second class was with Professor Schier," he notes. As a result, his first meeting with Wise was at the suggestion of Professor Venderzell. "I hadn't met Professor Wise, but I had gotten an internship because I had grown up in New York with Alfonse D'Amato and Joe DioGuardi. I went to Professor Wise on a recommendation by Professor Vanderzell to figure out which one to take, and we sat down."

"I remember going into Sid's office in Goethean Hall, and his pulling out the *American Almanac of American Politics*, pulling out D'Amato's record and DioGuardi's record. He said to me, 'Look, you want to go somewhere where eventually people will remember that this guy either served or is serving, and it will serve you no purpose if this guy – if you go work there and then the guy gets defeated . He looked at both records and he said, 'This guy, D'Amato, of course, he's gonna clearly win in '86 and DioGuardi, I'm not quite sure about.' and he was right. DioGuardi lost in '88, if I remember correctly and D'Amato served all the way until '93, and to this day, I still run into people that I interned with in the D'Amato office, and so that was the first time I met Sid Wise, his giving me that sound political advice."

Blyth eventually took one course with Professor Wise, "his quintessential class, which was Congress," he remembers. "He steered me to write a paper on the line-item veto, an issue that's still discussed today, and he clearly solidified my deep love and interest in Congress. He was one of those John Houseman kind of professors from *The Paper Chase*, who just grabs you and pulls you in and defines your career."

Blyth's relationship with Professor Wise continued after graduation. "I think he really kind of forced me to figure out that your future does not lie where you think it does," says Blyth. "Your future lies somewhere else and it includes bigger and better things. I remember distinctly after I graduated, I went to work for the Navy for about nine months. It was my first job down here and for about a year and a half, maybe two years, Sid was very standoffish, and I think he did that on purpose." Over time, Blyth's relationship with Sid Wise changed. "I think you always look at your professors as professors, and you don't really look at them as colleagues, and I think at some point, I realized

209

that my tutelage is over and now you're a colleague of mine."

Perhaps Blyth's most important role in Sid Wise's Washington was keeping track of all of the F&M alumni on Capitol Hill. "I served 13 years on the Hill, but for at least ten years, Sid gave me the responsibility to find every F&M grad who was working on Capitol Hill. About every six months, I would go out with a list and double check and see who was working there. It was always very hard. It was all kind of hearsay and I was always shocked that it broke down 50/50 Democrat or Republican every single time. "

After Wise died, "Franklin & Marshall College called and said that they were establishing the Sid Wise Internship [for Public Service]. They asked me to be one of the first people to have a Sid Wise intern, and I said, 'Done, it's completely done.' That's when I worked for [Congressman] Bill Martini, and so we had the first Sid Wise intern in that Congressional office."

Wise's influence goes much farther, and has impacted every aspect of how Blyth runs a Congressional office. "I really wanted to have diverse staff in the respect that they were willing to represent the member's decision when they made that decision, but [were] willing to argue on what was positive and what was negative when thinking about it. He taught me that as well.

"This is what F&M taught you. When you reflect upon the framers, they were very practical individuals. From the Constitutional Conventions and the Declaration of Independence, if you go back and look at the history of the documents and the men who served, they were realists," Blyth explains. "They were practical and the fringes of any party never get anything done. It's the middle or the right of middle and sometimes to the left of middle that get things done. There are plenty of ideologues on Capitol Hill who go up there and stamp their feet and pound to the death, but at the end of the day, they don't really get very much done. It's the people who are the realists, and people in government who realize that you have to be practical, who get things done."

Blyth also acquired his appreciation of public service from Wise and his colleagues. "He also taught us that this is what we're supposed to do as F& M alumni. He taught us that it's not about the grades you get in politics. It's about the connections that you make, and the fact is, he had no enemies. He wasn't at all partisan; he interacted with Ken Duberstein, Bill Gray, Ken Mehlman and Dan Turton [who served in the White House Office of Legislative Affairs under President Obama]. [His connections] reached the highest level of each political party," says Blyth.

"Whenever an F&M student calls me – I'm going to help you. I counsel some of them for years to push them, the same way he pushed all of us. I think you always wanted to do it because for everything he had done for you, but you also knew it was the right thing to do," concludes Blyth.

# F&M Government Department Timeline

- •1853: First free-standing course related to politics offered
- •1915: Degree in politics offered, with one faculty member
- •1928: Dept. of Political Science created
- •1950: Program graduates seven students
- •1952: Sid Wise, John Vanderzell join faculty
- •1953: Dick Schier joins faculty
- •1955: Department renamed Government Department
- •1966: Stan Michalak joins faculty
- •1969: Program graduates 57 students
- •1970: Grier Stephenson, Joe Karlesky join faculty
- •1972: Bob Gray joins faculty
- •1976: Bob Friedrich joins faculty

**The Big Three:**
**John Vanderzell, Sid Wise & Richard Schier**

# A Tribute to Sidney Wise

By Professor Robert Friedrich

F&M Washington Alumni Gathering
Washington Hilton
September 1, 1988

It is a pleasure to speak to so many distinguished alumni of the College, many of whom owe your success at least in part to the counsel and assistance – yes, even the letters, phone calls, and other personal interventions – of Sidney Wise. I want to commend you for having the good sense not to wear your National Guard uniforms tonight.

One of the most remarkable things about Sidney Wise is the range of his involvements -the incredible variety of things he has done over his 36 years at the College. It is more than one could ever hope to list, much less properly acknowledge, in the time we have tonight. Fortunately, Sidney will be honored on many other occasions this year. Thus I will leave it to other people in other places at other times to talk about such things as:

- Sidney and Eileen and the graciousness and hospitality they have shown to so many of us over the years;

- Sidney and the rise of the Government Department as we know it at F&M;

- Sidney and movies -excuse me, Sidney, film;

- Sidney and the media;

- Sidney and Lancaster politics;

- Sidney and the American Political Science Association (at whose convention we gather tonight);

- Sidney and College governance;

- Sidney and all the speakers he has brought to campus;

- Sidney and the College Reporter;

- Sidney and the College Democrats – and Republicans

- Sidney and the career forums;

- Sidney and commencement speakers;

- Sidney and College presidents;

- Sidney and his experience working in state and federal government;

I could go on and on. Rather, it seems appropriate in this city on this night with this group of people to focus on three related things: Sidney and politics, Sidney and his role as a mentor, and Sidney and people.

## I.  Sidney and Politics

Sidney Wise loves politics. In part it is because he has such affection for people in general and the people of politics in particular, people he is willing to assume are people of good character and good will until shown otherwise.

Sidney respects political institutions and, in general, the way things are because he knows that there are often good reasons why things are the way they are. Some would say that this makes Sidney a conservative. But just last Saturday Sidney clarified this. He was asked to address a Mayser Gym full of new freshmen and their parents on the pursuit of liberal education and, of course, he hit the ball out of the park. One piece of advice he gave them was this: "Don't try to change something until you understand it."

Presented to an audience of college freshmen, this is profoundly conservative advice. But presented to good students or experienced alumni, it is strategy and even (pardon the trendy word) empowerment. For a person of Sidney's intelligence and experience-on campus, in Lancaster, in Harrisburg, and in Washington, it translates into political power of real consequence - power because Sidney knows so much about how things work and is so good at translating that understanding into action. Sidney knows when things need to be changed and Sidney knows how to change them.

## II.    Sidney as Mentor

All this leads me to Sidney as mentor: because Sidney loves politics and believes politics is an honorable calling, he wants to encourage good people to go into politics.

A few weeks ago Joe Karlesky moved back into Goethean Hall, next door to Sidney's office, after several years away as Associate Dean and on sabbatical. He told me how he was struck by the constant flow of people through Sidney's office, like the waiting room to Don Corleone's inner chamber, he said. Anybody who has spent any time around the Government Department or ever dropped in to talk to Sidney will know exactly what Joe was talking about-a constant succession of students, former students, future students and their parents, faculty, friends, reporters, and College administrators. The diversity of the visitors speaks eloquently to the range of matters on which Sidney's expertise is recognized and his advice is valued.

But certainly much of the traffic in the hall and conversation on the phone has to do with what the *New York Times* last year called the "network." Tonight we could just call it "good jobs at good wages," or perhaps more accurately, "good jobs at government wages," or even more accurately "good internships at no wages at all."

All these job-related comings and goings remind me a little of Margaret Leech's description, in a fine book called *Reveille in Washington*, of the White House and patronage in the first days of the Lincoln Administration. Let me quote:

> The [job] seekers, ravenous for post-offices, consulates, and Indian agencies, had immediately taken possession of the White House. They occupied the parlors and halls, and loitered on the portico and lawns. The anteroom of the President's office and the second-floor corridor were filled with restless applicants, bristling with credentials. At all hours of the day,

two queues moved on the broad staircase,
one going up, the other corning down.

Now that is not a totally accurate description of Sidney's office. Sidney's office is on the first floor.

The *New York Times* says: 145 former Wise students in Washington, "perhaps one of the largest networks of protégés in the nation's capitol"-145 students from a small liberal arts college in Lancaster County, Pennsylvania. To quote John Vanderzell, "Wow!" And to bring it home tonight: How many of the people in this room tonight would be here if it were not for Sidney Wise? Sidney, you should be very proud.

Many of us will feel this loss of Sidney as a mentor in a profound way. How many of us have, when confronted with a personal or professional or political crisis, sought out Sidney's advice or help or reassurance? Take, for example, me tonight. Previously, when I've had to speak at some important occasion like this, I've gone and bounced what I thought I would say off Sidney. But I really didn't think I could do that for tonight. My only consolation is that I am just the first of many who will have to learn to operate in this vacuum.

## III. Sidney and People

Finally, Sidney and people. Why do all these people come to Sidney? That has to do with the kind of person Sidney is. He is sympathetic, caring, and, of course, funny. One of my earliest memories of Sidney is bumping into him coming out of the College Center my first semester at F&M. He had the biggest box of Kleenex I have ever seen under his arm. "Are you getting a cold?"

I asked him. "No," he replied drily, "I'm giving back freshman midterms today."

Sidney is generous with his time and patient with those of us who still have a lot to learn. He is intelligent and well-read, a voracious reader-and watcher, an unabashed yet unpretentious intellectual, and as shrewd as they come. When George Washington Plunkitt of Tammany Hall inveighed against "bookworms and college professors and philosophers who go up in a balloon to think," he could have done so only because Sidney Wise hadn't been born yet. And when Sidney was born, I can only conclude he was born a politician, born a mentor, and born a teacher.

Finally, I don't know of anybody who loves the College more or truly always thinks of what is best for the College than does Sidney Wise -not what is best for some person or some department or some group, but for the College. Nor do I know of anybody who has done more for the College. In talking to others about Sidney, you quickly learn that, while you think you know everything Sidney has done, you don't know the half of it. And, remarkably, the people you talk to learn the same thing from you.

***

It is customary to end remarks like these with a burst of optimism and a pledge to carry on the work of the retiring colleague. We are all optimistic about the future of the department and of the College. But it is not exaggerating to say that things will never be the same. I will use two clichés which, because I am talking about Sidney, transcend cliché: Sidney is one of a kind and we will not see his likes again. When a colleague retires, it is customary also to say thanks for years of service. But I think in this case it goes beyond that: most of us in this room are in one way or another personally, individually, in Sidney's debt. For everything Sidney has done to touch us, to enrich our lives and our learning, we each and all of us say thank you-and offer our best wishes to you and Eileen for the year ahead and the years after.

One last note: I said that I had not talked to Sidney about what I would say here tonight. But I know I have Sidney's approval for concluding these remarks by not asking you to join together in saying the Pledge of Allegiance.

# Remarks for Sidney Wise Memorial Service 2-22-94

By Richard Kneedler

Like many of you, I suspect, my years in association with Franklin & Marshall have been inextricably intertwined with one of the most appropriately named people I have ever met, Professor Wise.

Last Tuesday, I saw Sidney Wise at a luncheon for alumni in Sarasota, Florida. He was clearly having a good time. He told several of us that, were he but 65 again, he and Eileen would move to Florida. This from a man who had exhibited a high degree of skepticism about a first winter vacation there just a few years ago!

Sidney was especially happy because, that morning, he had met their daughter, Debby Booth, at the airport. She and their granddaughter, Anna, had just arrived for a few days of winter sunshine by the pool.

At the luncheon, Sidney talked with each of the alumni personally, shared memories and made everyone feel welcome. As always, he was the guest at the center of the party, making all of us feel special.

Sidney Wise was doing, that day, exactly what he wanted to do and he was happy in a most perfect fashion doing it. That was always my impression of Sidney that he was doing what he wanted...talking and teaching about political science and films, thinking about and following the careers of the students whose lives, happily, had intersected with his, over 40 years with this College (most recently as our number one alumni volunteer), and, most of all, being with Eileen and, as often as possible, the family that they both adored.

At that luncheon in Sarasota, Sidney mentioned how perfect their winter place was. After all, he said, there was a little shop very nearby where he could get his New York Times every morning at seven. This lovely, modest man would have been astonished and, 1 suspect, moved that the newspaper around, which so much of his life focused would pay him the tribute that it did last Thursday. It said that he emphasized the human element of governing and I think he would have been happy describing his career by reference to all the students whom he had helped.

We are here today, family, friends, colleagues and students of Sidney Wise to remember someone special, really unique beyond the power of language to convey specialness. This memorial will proceed without further announcement. You are invited to greet Sidney's family, and each other, after the service, on the second floor of the Steinman College Center.

# Ken Duberstein Eulogy of Sid Wise

## February 22, 1994
## Lancaster, PA.

I am honored to be with so much family to salute a dear friend, to celebrate Sid Wise's life, and to say thank you on behalf of scores and scores of Franklin and Marshall graduates for inspiring each of us with his love of politics, public policy and public service.

He made a difference, a huge difference in our lives and the history of this college, this Commonwealth and I would suggest this country. We are the young men and women who went on from his classroom in Old Main to become Congressmen and State Reps, Hill staffers, White House assistants, judges, Supreme Court clerks, federal executive and state and local government managers. We are the Stan Brand's, the Al Zuck's, the Bill Gray's, the Jon Plebani's and the Les Lenkowsky's and so many others who were his students.

Sid Wise and his then colleagues Dick Schier, John Vanderzell and John Pittenger prepared us with not simply old theories but new realities. They were not Ivory tower professors but hands on pragmatists who understood that politics is about people and about achieving the art of the possible. They weren't ideologues; they were doers. They shared their love for the institution of governing. They prepared us for the rough and tumble of politics as a contact sport on the Hill, in the Administration or on TV fielding shouted questions from Sam Donaldson or Andrea Mitchell. After one of Sid's final exams, Sam's inquiries were virtual softballs.

And their mentoring didn't end at commencement. Upon graduation, I applied for a summer internship with my home state senator, Jacob Javits. With Sid's sponsorship, I was accepted only to discover that internships don't pay. Sid's answer was to say not to worry~ he might be able to get me a grant to cover living expenses. He did --$500 with only 2 requirements. Do well and come back to F&M, meet with the government club and talk to the next generation of students. I remember his words-"Maybe you can help some of them get jobs." He was relentless in his pursuit of opportunities for his fellas!

Through the years, Sid always remembered to keep in touch, to write, to inspire, to check on employment opportunities for new graduates, to be there for a needed "attaboy" or other prudent advice.

When I was chief of congressional liaison at the White House during President Reagan's first term, I received a letter from Sid urging me to sit down with another F&M graduate, then Congressman Bill Gray. It would be helpful to the country, he wrote, if you two would talk and understand one another. You represent different philosophies and different political parties. And you might even get his vote from time to time.

Bill received a similar note. We were on the phone immediately and frequently thereafter, especially when he had become Chairman of the Budget Committee and then Majority Whip, and I had returned to the White House as Deputy and then Chief of Staff. We had Sid Wise and F&M in common and a commitment to doing what was right. We agreed often and when we disagreed, we did so without being disagreeable. And yes, I got his vote occasionally but even when 1 didn't, public policy was enhanced by our dialogue.

As you can imagine, I'd often call Sid to ask his insights when some issue or vote was troubling me. What am I missing? Why's our strategy not working? How is it all playing in Lancaster? Sometimes I just called to kibitz, to just hear a friendly voice. Washington is a tough town, you know.

He was my secret weapon, my reality check. His observations were so often on target. But I remember one late evening when I was Chief of Staff, calling Sid to ask his advice on a particularly sensitive issue. Help me think this one through, I asked. 1 remember his chuckle. And he said, "Walt a minute. I don't have the answer. You're the professor. I'm the student now."

We laughed. He wrote me later when the events played out on the front pages of his beloved New York Times. He said, 'Well, you muddled through without me, kid. Well done."

Sid Wise was a mentor, a gentle statesman, a wise counselor, an uncommon friend. He is what a Franklin and Marshall education is all about. His commitment to each of his students was unmatched. His commitment to excellence unparalleled.

I have lost two heroes on February 15th, three years apart – my father and Sid Wise. I am thankful for their teachings and their love. I only hope that they are looking down on us today and saying I've done them proud. I've sure tried.

So, to Eileen, David and Debbie ---thank you, thank you for sharing Sid with us. He made a difference to so many of us during <u>his internship</u> here on earth. Now, he's surely advising a higher authority!

God bless.

# Joel Eigen

The conventional logic of a memorial service dictates that speakers come forward to represent various constituencies

-colleagues

-department members

-students

-and my group ... friends & faculty.

But we are dealing here with a most unconventional,

a most singular man

and the conventional logic of separate constituencies simply doesn't hold. –

-the lines are blurred for all of us who knew, respected, and admired Sidney.

I was not his student, but he was my teacher.

I was not in his department, but he was my chair

I was not in in his family, but he was the wise and patient uncle I often needed.

Where is the line

between friend and colleague

between a trusted advisor and a confidante

The reason why these boundaries are so indistinct, is that

long before there were the buzz-words of contemporary education,

-nurturer

226

-mentor

-role model

There was Sidney

How many of us came to the faculty without a clue of what it meant to be

a member of such a body

A practitioner of the art of teaching? The instructors of youth?

How many of our cohorts in Graduate School could have hoped to find

on their arrival an educator's educator

a man who lit the path both for students and for the young

practitioner of the art?

Not by didactic indoctrination

not by endless appeal to caring

but through an unshakable conviction that we were the trustees of

our students' education

and that responsibility was a sacred one.

How was he so effective at imparting this message?

I suspect that few of us realized how much his friendship was the conduit for the

lessons of what it meant to be to take one's place on the faculty ...

And what a gift for friendship he had.

In talking about Sidney with Mike Roth and Sandy Pinsker,

I discovered that what I had always considered to be a singular experience

was indeed shared by many.

One night, in a fury over some business at the College

I stormed back to my office

dialed 397-8265

and was summarily summoned to 810 Race Avenue.

Little did I know that this was hardly a novel thought

I was in fact following a well-worn route to the one person,

the only person, who could have possibly wound me down . .

Ushered into the living room

Sidney took what I have since learned was his usual spot in the wing chair nearest

the bookshelf

Eileen offered coffee, then returned to the living room sofa, to offer her own sage

counsel

And Sid listened patiently

-finally venturing forth with

Joel, Joel..now now

What is it about a person, that in moments of despair and distress,

without anyone telling you that he is the person to call

you simply realize ... he is the person to call.

228

But he was more than the person who listened

He was the friend who did what only the most significant friends will do

-compel you to look within yourself for the answer... to understand that

there was more at stake than your problems,

there was certainly more at stake than your feeling _good_ about yourself

there was yet something else to think about.

And that something else was also present in the living room.

Along with you, and Eileen, and Sidney

There was the College.

He understood how precious, and binding was the purpose

that drew us one to another

that led us to recognize a commitment to free inquiry into what

was true; what was good; and what was honorable

free that is, of ideology and agendas.

Sidney understood that what unites us -a respect for the privilege and the

responsibility of the podium-

was unfathomably greater and more sustaining

than what divides on any one issue

He trusted that his values were shared by us,

and so he counseled to stay the course

to resist fad and fashion

to resist the trendy to pursue the transcendent.

All of this he was able to impart with his friendship and exemplary teaching.

Like the best of old friends who reminds you who you were

Sidney reminded you to stick to the principles that propelled you into the

profession

He guided, he illuminated, he inspired.

There is a story about a trip that the Pinskers, the Deweys, The Roths, and the Wises took

to Washington,

including as a major objective -a tour of the White House.

In typical fashion, Sidney did not ask Ken Duberstein for a personal tour

he only asked when the best time would be to avoid the crowds.

Standing in a never-ending line filled with hundreds of people

the F&M party was understandably delighted when a guard approached and asked

if Professor Wise was present.

What followed, according to Mike, was the grandest of grand tour of the presidential

mansion

a guided gaze into the history and dignity of our nation's traditions.

How fitting that Sidney should have been treated
to a tour that he carved out for each of us

A guide who illuminated the dignity or
our calling, and **the history of its
traditions.**

As colleague, teacher, and ultimately friend,
Sid Wise enjoined us to pursue all that
was noble

and all that
would honor our College

Remarks at the Sid Wise Memorial,
Joel Eigen February 22, 1994

# Thanks for the memories ...

There is a story about a trip that the Pinskers, the Deweys, the Roths and the Wises took to Washington, including as a major objective a tour of the White House. In typical fashion, Sidney did not ask Ken Duberstein ('65, former chief of staff) for a personal tour, he only asked when the best time would be to avoid the crowds. Standing in a never-ending line filled with hundreds of people, the F&M party was understandably delighted when a guard approached and asked if Professor Wise was present. What followed, according to Mike (Roth), was the grandest of grand tours of the presidential mansion, a guided gaze into the history and dignity of our nation's traditions. How fitting that Sidney should have been treated to a tour that he carved out for each of us.

*-Joel Eigen, associate professor, sociology*

As some of you know, we rotate the chairmanship in the department of government, and we usually try to descend this chore upon the most recently tenured member. The transition usually goes like this: The keys to the file cabinet are handed over to the new chairman, and he is then told the following, "We're all around in case you need us; try to keep departmental meetings to no more than one per semester; and if you get something that's really tough or you can't figure out what to do, just ask Sidney. Well, we can't ask Sidney any more. Sadly, very sadly, but truly, we are now on our own.

*-Stanley Michalak, professor, government*

Sidney Wise was a remarkable combination of intelligence and wit, realism and idealism, intellectual toughness and generosity of spirit. He had more political sense and common sense and people sense than anybody I've ever met. He was intrigued by the way that institutions, especially political ones, worked and he revered institutions that worked well. Among the institutions he revered most was the College. Sidney Wise cared about Franklin & Marshall College more deeply than anybody I know. That's why to lose him and all the talents he put in service to the College leaves so many of us feeling such a void.

*-Robert J. Friedrich, associate professor,*
*government*

Sidney Wise was, for almost 40 years, the most nurturing professor at Franklin & Marshall. He cared about both the intellectual development and the lives of his students and his colleagues. He was a nationally recognized political scientist (serving on the board of the American Political Science Association), but it was his commitment to the College he loved and the students he guided that will live on for decades to come. Few institutions have anyone remotely like Sidney. All of us who knew and loved him will tell stories about his kindness, wisdom and integrity until the day we die.

*-Robert C. Gray, professor, government*

As you can imagine, I'd often call Sid to ask his insights when some issue or vote was troubling me. What am I missing? Why's our strategy not working? How is it all playing in Lancaster? Sometimes I called to kibitz, to just hear a friendly voice. Washington is a tough town, you know. He was my secret weapon, my reality check. His observations were so ⊓ often on target. But I remember one late evening when I was chief of staff calling Sid to ask his advice on a particularly sensitive issue. "Help me think this one through," I asked. I remember his chuckle. And he said, "Wait a minute. I don't have the answer. You're the professor. I'm the student now."

*-Ken Duberstein '65, former chief of staff to President Ronald Reagan*

I think Sid's influence on his students has been more profound, more personal and permanent than placing people in jobs. It's a special bond that we share. So often I would confront a tough issue and think about how Professor Wise might respond. Or I would observe or experience some crazy event in public life and chuckle about how Sid would get a kick out of it. Or I would recall a phrase and realize that's what he meant back in Gov. 24. And through phone calls, notes, news clips and rare visits we would stay in touch --although now, of course, I realize not nearly enough. How fortunate and extraordinary it was for all of us to remain so connected to him for so long ... To know Sid Wise was to respect him, to appreciate him, and to love him. And now, sadly, to miss him very much.

*-Debra Amper Kahn '75, member of the Philadelphia School Board*

# Eulogy for Sidney Wise

## Memorial Service • Franklin and Marshall College February 22, 1994

### By Debra Amper Kahn

I came to F&M for its radio station and to avoid phys ed. But I stayed--and thrived-because of Sid Wise.

His warmth and good humor were irresistible. His wholehearted interest in my work and my well-being was comforting and inspiring. His intense loyalty to this College was contagious. His challenging teaching kept me signing up for more. And his passion that politics and government were admirable, doable, and fun sparked in me and countless others a commitment to public service that would shape our lives.

Looking back I have come to realize that Professor Wise had a master plan for many of his students. He certainly did for me, from the selection of a major, to the subject for my honors thesis, to the choice of a graduate school. But his genius, I think, in advising know-it-all college students, was to make you believe that all of the ideas were yours alone.

The four brief years spent on campus with Sid Wise made a mountain of lasting memories: mind-stretching, hand-numbing final exams; Friday afternoon chats in Old Main featuring his pithy commentary on current events; celebrity meetings, including a limousine ride from Washington to Lancaster with Ben Bradlee during the height of Watergate; parent visits when a conversation with Professor Wise always reassured them they were getting their tuition' s worth; and many a dull weekend saved thanks to his fabulous film series.

But lucky for me, this was just the start of a beautiful friendship.

Sid Wise's involvement with his students didn't end upon graduation. He was renowned for his ingenuity and effectiveness in helping so many of his best and brightest find employment. But let me say for the record, that while The New York Times may have chosen to remember him for creating an "old boys' network" on Capitol Hill, in Sid Wise's world "new girls" definitely need apply

Still, I think Sid's influence on his students has been more profound, more personal and permanent than placing people in jobs. It's a special bond that we share. So often I would confront a tough issue and think about how Professor Wise might respond. Or I would observe or experience some crazy event in public life and chuckle about how Sid would get a kick out of it. Or I would recall a phrase and realize that's what he meant back in Gov. 24. And through phone calls, notes, news clips and rare visits we would stay in touch--although now, of course, I realize not nearly enough. How fortunate and extraordinary it was for all of us to remain so connected to him for so long

There is a Yiddish word that I think best describes how Sid felt about and acted towards his students. The word is "kvel"; is a verb which roughly translated means to glow with pride, to take tremendous pleasure from, even to boast a bit about the source of that joy. And that's what Sid did: he kvelled from our academic achievements, our personal milestones with spouses and children, and our career successes. He never tired of telling us about how others were doing, all the while making each of us feel very special in our own right. And he never let on that he might have had at least a little something to do with any of our accomplishments.

To know Sid Wise was to respect him, to appreciate him, and to love him. And now, sadly, to miss him very much.

# A Tribute to Sidney Wise

by

Stanley Michalak

February 22, 1994

In 1947, officials at the Ford Foundation joined in creating the Citizenship Clearing House. The Clearing House's mission was a simple one: to fund programs that would get the nation's brightest undergraduates interested and working in practical politics.

By the late 1950s, students were dining and rapping with mayors, county commissioners, local legislators, congressmen and even Senators occasionally. In addition, student interns were turning up in party and government offices at the city, county, state, and national levels.

Sidney Wise was centrally involved in this national effort from the very beginning of his career. In fact, my earliest meeting with Sidney occurred in April of 1959. I and six other political science majors from Albright College attended a dinner along with majors from other regional colleges at the old Royal House on Duke and Lime Streets. We were there to find out how a man named Tom Monaghan managed to become Lancaster's first Democratic mayor in longer than anyone could remember. The event, of course, was Sidney's, but little did I know how much he had to do with the political upset as well.

Within\a few years Sidney was the Director of the Pennsylvania Branch of CCH, and by the mid-sixties, the Pennsylvania branch had the nation's largest internship program.

The purpose of it all was well put by Sidney: "to encourage young people to enter the most meaningful political channel of all---partisan politics."

When the foundations moved on to other worthy purposes, Sidney and his colleagues continued on at F&M--teaching students about what politics was really like, placing them into politicians' offices, hitching them up with elected officials and their staffs, keeping them in touch with one another, and, of course, bringing them back to campus to talk with the current crop of students.

I am telling you all of this for a very important reason: those hundreds and hundreds of graduates out there in public life are not there because of some accident or some whim or some idiosyncrasy of Sidney Wise. They are out there because Sidney and his colleagues, Dick Schier and John Vanderzell, made explicit choices.

In their opinion, the job of undergraduate colleges was to educate citizens in the largest sense of that term. As Dick Schier succinctly put it, "Our entire Department stresses the concept of public service."

Sidney Wise chose to make his students and their development the center of his life--and he considered himself a professor, not a scholar. He worried less about his national reputation than he did about the reputation of the students who left his charge He placed his primary loyalty not to his academic discipline but to this institution, Franklin and Marshall College.

His was a different culture with a very different mission.

But as all of you do know very well, Sidney was not merely a professor with a sense of vocation. Sidney Wise was also an absolutely brilliant and masterful political analyst. Whether it was a campus issue or some weighty national political controversy, Sidney could spin out ironies, insights, dubious assumptions, and situational dilemmas with a speed that left the rest of us breathless.

And did he have style. Grier Stephenson was not exaggerating when he quipped that Sidney had elevated the *wise*crack to an entirely new plane-and yes, the pun was intended.

Sidney was also a flawless administrator and consummate practitioner of that meanest and nastiest of all politics--college politics; mean, nasty, and vile, as Sydney frequently reminded us, because .the stakes were always so small.

As some of you know, we rotate the chairmanship in the Department of Government, and we usually try to descend this chore upon the most recently tenured member.

The transition usually goes like this: The keys to the file cabinet are handed over to the new chairman, and be is then told the following, "We're all around in case you need us; try to keep departmental meetings to no more than one per semester; and if you get

240

something that's really tough or you can't figure out what to do, just ask Sidney. Well, we can't ask to Sidney any more. Sadly, very sadly, but truly, we are now on our own.

Almost thirty years ago, Sidney Wise asked me if I would consider joining the Department of Government at Franklin and Marshall College.

But even then, my relationship with Sidney was not a recent one. When I was an undergraduate congressional intern in the summer of 1959, Sidney and I talked about politics on several occasions. That internship, that dinner at the Royal House, those meetings with politicians in Philadelphia and Harrisburg --these significantly shaped my decision to go on to graduate school rather than law school.

At the end of my first semester in graduate school, my local Congressman asked if I would become his legislative assistant when the new Congress assembled in January of 1961. Thanks to that CCH internship, I had that contact. Obviously, I put graduate school on hold--especially so since the new Kennedy administration would be hitting the ground.

So in February of 1961, I got onto a Trailways bus with a beat up old suit case; off I was to join the New Frontier. Within a matter of weeks, Sidney Wise came into the office. He was now running the internship program for Eastern Pennsylvania. Would we take a summer intern? You bet.

Over the next year and half, Sid and I got together whenever he was in Washington. When I later taught at Ohio State, we would have lunch at Kegel's, whenever I drove to my parents' home for vacation.

When Sidney Wise offered me the chance to work with him as a colleague, I knew exactly what an opportunity stood before me. What an offer. What a compliment. I couldn't have been more flattered by an invitation from any other place but his own alma mater.

And for the past twenty eight years, I have been truly blessed with colleagues who have enriched my life beyond exaggeration and students who made a life of teaching a challenge and a pleasure.

If ever a person was truly at home, I have been at home at this college and so much of that is due to the Sidney Wise--a person who has had more of an impact on my life than any other man except for my father.

We in the Department will miss him always, for we shall not see the likes of him again.

# Dedication of the Sidney Wise Plaque

Charles Leayman, F & M Film Series, 4/13/1995

I find it amazing how accurately the photograph on the plaque donated by Mrs. Schaffner in memory of Sidney Wise captures something of the man's particular qualities. In spirited conversation with Franklin Schaffner, Sidney's customary casualness doesn't conceal the respect he holds for his partner: respect for Mr. Schaffner's intelligence, sensibility, and supremely competent craft. It's a respect that, in this case, Sidney often articulated, whether to his film studies students or to friends and colleagues who shared his enthusiasm for Mr. Schaffner's impressive work.

At the same time, however, there is no sense of obsequiousness or fawning in the presence of a celebrity. Sidney always retained an assured sense of his own professionalism, whether as an educator, mentor, or behind-the-scenes mover and shaker on Capitol Hill. Like the characters in the films of director Howard Hawks (whose unpretentiousness and simplicity of technique he much admired), Sidney's confidence in his abilities precluded the need for advertising them. And linked to this was an unfailing generosity toward the achievements of others: a penchant, indeed an eagerness, to celebrate the victories of others and to encourage their aspirations (whether these took the form of an internship in Washington or a film director's dreams of the movies still to be made).

As always with Sidney, humor was never far from his lips. Perhaps it stems simply from the years of relishing Sidney's understated but often ferociously funny wit, but I can't look at that picture without detecting behind those eyes the wonderful sense of irony that made Dr. Wise such an enjoyable table companion and conversationalist. His comments were frequently barbed (particularly when he was talking politics), but I never knew them to be cruel or vindictive. When it came to movies, there were more than a few filmmakers whose work he simply didn't like, but because of his knowledge of and respect for the complex craft of making film s and the reservoirs of money and energy it consumed, Sidney more often than not laced his criticisms with a diplomacy worthy of a statesman. (One notable exception: when Brian De Palma released his -for its time -ultra-violent remake of "Scarface," Dr. Wise didn't hesitate on several occasions to remark that "the man should be run out of the business," uttered with an invincible conviction that invited no argument).

Finally, in the exchange depicted between Sidney and Franklin Schaffner, one can almost hear the enthusiasm that Sidney exuded when he talked about movies and movie-making. He had the gift that certain film critics possess (for example, Andrew Sarris and Pauline Kael) of making you want to rush out, after reading or hearing them, and SEE MOVIES! Sidney never seemed to lose that singular excitement some of us once felt when the lights went down and a massive curtain parted or rose on what we hoped would be a thrilling experience. And for all his ability to hold his own with a man of Mr. Schaffner's stature, I suspect that he never entirely abandoned that primal, childlike fascination that movie lovers share for the artists who make the pictures move.

244

And if further proof of this were needed, I can recall the comments made over the years by students who took Dr. Wise's class on the history of American film. These were undergraduates who were hardly experts on the refinements of cinematic technique, but more than one enthused about how Sidney's course had helped her or him to experience movies in a new way, not only with an appreciation for the tradition from which they sprang, but more importantly with an increased sophistication in seeing and hearing and evaluating what appeared before them, both on-and off-screen. Not to mention the sheer fun that many attested to having in the class! (On the other hand, those unfortunates who took the class thinking it would be the proverbial "piece of cake," soon found that if watching movies was easy, taking Sidney's mid-terms and finals was anything but!)

It goes without saying that for over three decades Sidney *was* the Weekend Film Series, nurturing it from its once-a-week 16 mm beginnings in 1953, through the peak attendance years of the 1960s and early '70s when films and their auteurs were the medium and artists of choice for a generation of film enthusiasts, and undergraduates regularly packed Hensel Hall to see the latest works by Truffaut and Bergman, and to sample the cinemas of far-flung countries in what can only be viewed in retrospect as the first stirrings of the multinational awareness that has become a touchstone of our academic moment. Indeed, by the time Dr. Wise passed the film series mantle on to me in 1986, the twice-and sometimes four-times weekly screenings had become a staple of the college and community's cultural life, and an oasis in

Lancaster for unusual or foreign films that might otherwise never have shown locally.

Like Mr. Schaffner, Dr. Wise had very little tolerance for cant and jargon, especially where movies were concerned. The quickest way to squelch discussion with Mr. Schaffner was to attempt to impose on his work some high-flown *auteurist* rationale or heavily academic interpretation; he was too much the team player, and too respectful of his frequently used colleagues, to ever impute a film's dynamism solely to himself. Sidney for his part had little truck with the Continental theories like structuralism and semiotics that began to seep into film studies by the end of the '60s, along with massive incursions by psychoanalysis and feminism, before becoming an academic cottage industry throughout the '70s and '80s, when the cultural buzzwords were "deconstruction" and "postmodernism." I, on the other hand, loved these developments and was only too willing to discuss them with the person who was not only a friend and film series mentor, but a man whose excitement over movies matched my own. I can still see Sidney rolling his eyes and chuckling quietly when I would drop references to "Lacan," or "Althusser," or "Raymond Bellour" (all critical big guns at the time), hoping to convince him of their merit. I don't think I ever succeeded, but the beauty part was that Sidney, while not abandoning his skepticism about this "critical theory" that I loved to bedevil him with (along with my love for low-grade horror movies), never once urged me not to read such writers and may even have dipped into them on his own as he sensed the sea change occurring in the study of films.

When Sidney officially retired from the Weekend Film Series in 1986, a major shift in the viewing habits of moviegoers had already begun, triggered by the advent of home video players, escalating television channels, and a tremendously increased circulation of the kind of films that once would have played locally solely under the Film Series' auspices. Video essentially privatized the viewing of movies, drawing people from theatres and confining them to the living room and the dorm room. In addition the moment of cinema's cultural ascendancy passed, eclipsed by TV, rock music, and video itself. Undergraduates not only passed up the latest Antonioni for MTV, but didn't even know who Antonioni was.

But for those who knew Dr. Wise through the series and the classroom, or better still as a friend, Sidney played a major role both in refining the love for movies in those of us who seemingly possessed it from birth, and in igniting it in others by enabling them to see and hear, and thus to feel, in exciting new ways. He did it through knowledge, humor, generosity, and though it sounds archaic to say it, through a sense of mission. Sidney believed in movies, and he believed in people, and he loved bringing the two together.

On behalf of the Weekend Film Series, and on behalf of the many people whose lives touched and were touched by it, I wish to thank Mrs. Schaffner for her gift and for contributing to keeping alive the memory of a marvelous man.

Thank you.